New British Architecture

New British Architecture

Jonathan Glancey

With 172 illustrations, 24 in color

Thames and Hudson

The publishers would like to thank Design Analysis International for their help in producing this book.

First published in the United States in 1990 by Thames and Hudson Inc., 500 Fifth Avenue, New York, New York 10110

Library of Congress Catalog Card Number 89–50627

Printed and bound in Singapore

Contents

Contents

Chapter Five   133

Shops

Chapter Six   147

Industrial Buildings

Chapter Seven   163

Urbanism

Introduction

After more than twenty years of not-so-splendid isolation, British architects have begun to form a fresh relationship with the public in the 1980s. The *bêtes noires* of the 1960s, associated by the public with unsympathetic high-rise housing, insensitive office developments and bunker-like art galleries, architects have started to emerge from their protective professional shell. Throughout the decade many British architects have begun to re-examine history, to look afresh at the effects of modern building and planning on city centres, to reconsider the notion of decoration. Whether designing High-Tech offices such as Foster Associates' Hongkong and Shanghai Bank, country houses like John Outram's Palladian-inspired villa in Sussex (pp. 52-57) or avant-garde shops like Branson and Coates's shop Silver (p. 34), architects have begun to employ the wealth of new craft skills that have emerged over the decade. Architecture is taking its place in the popular imagination, where it rightfully belongs.

The shift from the welfare state of the 1950s to the hard-edged enterprise economy of the 1980s has also meant that architects have had to respond directly to market forces, fashions and new building types. Sir Denys Lasdun (b. 1914), Britain's 'architect laureate', whose work includes the National Theatre (1967-77; p. 20) and the Royal College of Physicians in London, has begun his first speculative city office building in the late 1980s after half a century in practice. This is a significant change from previous decades; until the decline of the public sector in the mid-1970s, architects like Lasdun were given grand commissions by the state, local authorities or the new universities.

The collapse of the British economy in the winter of 1973/74, an event which helped to bring down the Conservative government of Edward Heath (1970-74), meant that work in the public sector dried up. Just as the large housing estates, inspired by Le Corbusier's drawings and polemics,

were becoming the focus of bitter hostility in the media and among community action groups, the crisis in the economy ensured that this type of project never left the drawing board again. Since the economic revival under the ideologically right-wing government of Margaret Thatcher in the 1980s, most architectural commissions have been in the heterogeneous private sector. Even if not as part of an inevitable process, the explosion of architectural styles has certainly coincided with the revitalization of the private sector.

In a much-quoted television interview in 1983, the Prime Minister, Margaret Thatcher, called for a return to Victorian values, by which she meant self-help, thrift, the strengthening of family ties, hard work and dutiful behaviour. By chance, the historian J. Mordaunt Crook saw an analogy between the new styles erupting in British architecture: in *The Dilemma of Style* (1987), Crook drew parallels between the collapse of Modernist certainties in the 1970s and 1980s and both the rise of the Picturesque movement in the late eighteenth century and late nineteenth-century Free Style eclecticism. In both periods, Crook argued, a dominant mode of architectural thinking was undermined: chaste, mathematical Palladianism in the eighteenth century and archaeologically correct Gothic Revival in the nineteenth. However, such comparisons are not easy to make in reality. Whereas these earlier stylistic revolutions had been inspired by literary, philosophical, artistic and political initiatives, the decline of Modern architecture over the past two decades has been brought about as much by economic circumstances as by its failure to win over a loyal public.

Between 1973 and the early 1980s, there were precious few commissions for Britain's most talented architects. James Stirling, famous the world over for such buildings as the popular Stuttgart Staatsgalerie (1977-84; p. 32), had been busy throughout the 1960s. After the sudden exit of Edward Heath from 10 Downing Street in January

1974, and for the best part of the next decade, Stirling carried out virtually no new work in Britain. Young architects qualifying at the time of the economic depression of the 1970s, during the Labour administrations of Harold Wilson (1974-76) and James Callaghan (1976-79), had virtually no chance of practising at all unless they looked abroad, or were prepared to work on the design of speculative office blocks, the refurbishment of existing buildings, or out-of-town leisure centres and hypermarkets which increased in number as unemployment rose.

The recession of the 1970s might have put a stop to projects from the most gifted architects, young and experienced alike, but at the very least it did give the profession a chance to reflect on the direction of modern architecture. The 1970s were years which saw a reappraisal of Modernism, a fresh understanding of urban design, of history and conservation, a return to decoration and, significantly, to drawing.

The fact that many of today's most accomplished young architects are working on the design of bars and cafés, shops and nightclubs, is not indicative of the scale of their ambition, but a reflection of economic circumstances. Had they been born thirty years earlier, architects like Nigel Coates (b. 1949), David Chipperfield (b. 1953) and Rick Mather (b. 1937) could well have been working for a public body such as the London County Council Architect's Department. Nowadays, after an apprenticeship in bars, cafés and small office conversions, they are being invited to design speculative offices in London, multi-use shopping and leisure developments in Tokyo, and hugely expensive apartment blocks for city professionals. The fact that their eclectic work is celebrated in the pages of fashion magazines and Sunday newspaper supplements makes an older generation of architects, brought up with Modernist certainties, wince. Yet, such press coverage means that architects are communicating with those to whom they

are ultimately responsible – the public at large. There has been an increasing recognition in the 1980s that buildings are not designed simply to satisfy the demands of the client but also to fulfil the needs of the public and the site.

Architecture and Morality

Apart from reappraising Modernism, architects in the 1980s have begun to reinterpret history. One of the slim, but influential, books that heralded the 1980s was David Watkin's *Morality and Architecture* (1977). In it Watkin attempted to undermine the essentially Victorian notion, propounded by the Gothic Revival architect A. W. Pugin (1812-52) and championed by the great art critic John Ruskin (1819-1900), that a particular approach to architecture could be morally right. Just as Pugin had believed Gothic to be the only morally correct style for British architecture, so Pevsner and many self-righteous architects in the twenty years after the Second World War believed Modernism to be the only true creed. The discovery by many architects in the 1970s that architecture could be a profound and responsible game played on many levels, rather than a moral crusade, freed approaches to design radically in the following decade. The significant exhibition 'The Presence of the Past' (1980), held in the Venice Arsenale, also opened the way to new connections between history and contemporary architecture. In England, the rehabilitation of Sir Edwin Lutyens (1869-1944) – a major retrospective was held at the Hayward Gallery, London, in 1981 – was another step away from Modernist dogma and towards a more pragmatic approach to architectural design.

The danger of ill-digested historical revivals and misconstrued Post-Modernism, however, made itself known in a rash of ill-informed commercial buildings which spread across the country from the late 1970s: shopping centres dressed in polychrome brickwork topped with Gothic towers or even, as in a 1987 proposal by the architects Chapman Taylor and Partners, built in the form of a collosal Palladian villa. It became easy to see why the youngest architects began to look back enthusiastically to the early work of Le Corbusier and the masters of the Modern Movement. In the late 1980s, a Modernist revival free from guilt and moral stricture is beginning to emerge. Yet the most significant pointer towards the future has been the gradual fusion of history, urbanism and craft with new technology, pragmatism and the most valuable lessons from the Modern experience. Since their attempt to make a clean break with the past after 1945, architects have begun to view their work as part of a continuous thread of historical development.

The changes in architectural thinking have been as dramatic as those in the British economy. In the late 1960s the triumph of Modern architecture in Britain had seemed complete. Apart from a few recalcitrant architects like Raymond Erith (1904-73) and Clough Williams-Ellis (1887-1978), who practised a late-flowering Classicism in rural backwaters, the architectural profession appeared, superficially at least, to have reached a concrete consensus. Architects who had dominated their profession before the Second World War with their Imperial Classicism, such as Sir Edwin Lutyens and Sir Herbert Baker (1862-1946), were not only forgotten, but wilfully excluded from histories of twentieth-century architecture written from a Modernist perspective. In Sir Nikolaus Pevsner's widely read *An Outline of European Architecture* (1943), there was no reference at all to Lutyens, one of Britain's most inventive and successful architects.

A German émigré and champion of Modern architecture, Pevsner selectively interpreted the history of late nineteenth-century and early twentieth-century British architecture as a gradual lead up to the full-blown Modernism achieved in the twenty years after 1945. This historicist perspective suggested that the rise of Modern architecture had been more or less inevitable. The industrial age required an appropriate machine-like architecture where the form of a building followed its function, while decoration drawing on past sources was strictly anathema. Modern architecture was not considered a style, but an appropriate response to the functional demands of twentieth-century life. To thousands of post-war British architects, Modernism offered certainty after a century of doubt. Since the demise of English Classicism in the 1840s, British architects had waged a 'battle of styles'. Grecian gave way to a studious Gothic revival in the 1840s, which in turn prised open a new Pandora's box. By the 1860s architects seemed free to indulge their wildest fantasies. Although the Arts and Crafts Movement championed by William Morris from the 1870s restrained many architects from decorative excess, there was still no universally accepted grammar of architecture – as there had been from the 1660s to the 1840s – until the rebuilding of Britain after the Second World War.

From the perspective of the mid-1960s, when the Modernist grip was at its most tenacious, this consensus approach to architecture seemed fully entrenched. The question of style appeared to have been resolved once and for all. Yet, in the 1980s, critics have been hard pressed to find labels that could satisfactorily categorize a heterogeneous approach to architectural form: the 'High Tech' or 'Late Modern' of Norman Foster, Richard Rogers, Michael Hopkins and Arup Associates; the 'Romantic Pragmatism' of Richard MacCormac and Edward Cullinan; the 'Neo-Classicism' of Quinlan Terry, Leon Krier, Robert Adam and John Simpson; the 'Post-Modernism' of Terry Farrell, John Outram and Jeremy Dixon; the 'Industrial Baroque' of Nigel Coates; or the 'Secular Modernism' (Modern forms re-examined and freed from the old morality) of Julyan

Wickham, David Chipperfield and Richard Horden. Historians such as David Watkin and Gavin Stamp have since argued that Modernism had never really taken root in Britain. A continental import, it was simply another style that was taken up when fashionable, and dropped when its image became tarnished in the 1970s.

The Pursuit of Perfection

Given the unpopularity of most Modern architecture built in the 1960s and early 1970s, perhaps it is surprising that architects continued to work in the idiom for so long. In fact, the reason was rooted deep in the architects' consciousness. Modern architecture was as much a moral crusade as a way of building. It was seen as morally good because it told no lies. The elevations of a Modern building were drawn straight from its plan. A Modern architect would never, so the theory went, deceive his public as Sir Christopher Wren (1632-1723) had done, for example, at St Paul's Cathedral where high Baroque walls hid a medieval Gothic plan, a narrow nave and flying buttresses. Modern architecture was morally right because it used materials honestly; no self-respecting Modern architect would pretend that one material was another. At the same time it was right because it sought to satisfy real, rather than imaginary, needs. *Existenzminimum* housing designed in Berlin by the German architects Walter Gropius (1883-1969) and Ludwig Mies van der Rohe (1886-1969) led the way by providing ceilings no more than seven foot high in apartments for factory workers. Why did anyone need more? 'Less', said Mies van der Rohe, 'is more.' (Forty years later the Post-Modern architect Robert Venturi would claim in riposte to Mies that 'Less is a bore'.) Modern architects condemned 'redundant space', any space inside a building superfluous to functional requirements. Finally, Modernism was right because it matched and mirrored the industrial world.

At its most extreme, Modern architecture was a puritanical, almost Calvinist mission. Perhaps the most influential of the early Modern Movement theorists was the Austrian architect Adolf Loos (1870-1933). His most memorable tract *Ornament und Verbrechen (Ornament and Crime)*, published in 1908, drew intriguing links between criminal behaviour and underworld decoration. The criminal classes were in the habit of covering their bodies in tattoos. No decent, upstanding citizen ever did this. By analogy, Loos argued that architects should divest their buildings of (immoral) decoration. A building, like a Greek temple, represented a high level of civilization because of its clear demonstration of pure, rational thought. (Ironically, as archaeological research had already proved by the time Loos wrote, the Parthenon was originally a blaze of bright colour and decoration.)

In the hands of purist architects such as Mies van der Rohe this approach could lead to a cold, Classical beauty, as found in the Prussian architect's German Pavilion for the International Exhibition in Barcelona (1928-29: reconstructed 1986) or the Neue Staatsgalerie, West Berlin (1962-68). Approached by an artist of genius like Le Corbusier (the pseudonym of Charles-Edouard Jeanneret, 1887-1965), Modern architecture was transformed through a complex framework of abstract ideas as challenging and as refreshing as the changing styles of his contemporary, Pablo Picasso. But, left to lesser talents, Modern architecture was almost guaranteed to fail, particularly when built quickly and cheaply by local authorities in a rush to provide as many rentable homes as possible and by property developers more concerned with maximizing office rents than with architectural quality. This was certainly the situation in Britain in the 1960s. Most Modern architects were unable to live up to the contradictory freedom and restraint that Modernism implied. Like other fundamentalist creeds, Modernism proved to be altogether too demanding for most architects, as it required them to approach each building anew, to determine the design by functional requirements, and to make the exterior a true reflection of the interior plan. Only in the hands of a consummate artist could such a demanding approach lead to great, or even likeable, architecture.

By contrast, the rudiments of the Classical language of architecture had been relatively easy to learn in the eighteenth century. Rural masons and big city property developers like Thomas Cubitt could easily follow precedents set out in readily available pattern books. As a consequence, Britain still boasts many handsome Georgian buildings, some the work of geniuses like Nicholas Hawksmoor (1661-1736) and Sir John Soane (1753-1837), but most simply the handiwork of self-taught builders following in such masters' footsteps. Despite the fact that architectural debate in the eighteenth century was acrimonious, arguments were settled within a set of given, and widely accepted, Classical rules.

However, the overlay of Modern architecture in the thirty years following the end of the Second World War has been less inspiring. Few architects have practised what they purport to preach. Few Modern buildings have been as 'honest' and as morally correct as they could have been: although expensive (because of their experimental nature), many are badly built; others seem deliberately ugly.

From Utopia to Toy Town

At first Modern architecture was associated with Utopian or Arcadian fantasies. Many young British architects, given the chance to design public housing in the twenty years following 1945, borrowed freely from Le Corbusier's vision of Modern cities featured in his highly influential books *Vers une Architecture* (1923; first published in Britain as *Towards a New Architecture*, 1927) and *La Ville radieuse* (1935; translated as *The Radiant City*, 1967).

Giant apartment blocks set in splendid isolation in verdant parkland on the edge of the city centre, connected by broad roads, would offer a new life to millions. High above the fast traffic, working-class families would enjoy nature and fresh air, exercising or sunbathing on their balconies. Run as tightly as an ocean liner, each residential block would be highly serviced, a liberating machine to live in.

Enthusiastic young British architects even aped the forms of Le Corbusier. The highly stylized, rough-cast concrete blocks that sit on the edge of Richmond Park, Surrey, and form the Roehampton estate (*below*) are testimony to an Arcadian dream that was never realized. The young architects working for the London County Council under the direction of Sir Leslie Martin (b. 1908) in the early 1950s might have had their hearts in the right place, but the cities Le Corbusier dreamed of would have been vastly expensive to build and to service. The Roehampton blocks formed a much-admired picturesque group, but lacked the amenities – and climate – that made Le Corbusier's Unité d'Habitation in Marseilles (1947-52) so popular with

The influence of Le Corbusier. Alton West estate, Roehampton, 1955-59, London County Council Architect's Department

professional as well as working-class families: safe places for children to play, rooftop swimming pool, shops and cafés incorporated into the block.

Built quickly and experimentally, although not always cheaply, British public housing of the 1950s and 1960s did much to destroy the credibility of the Modern Movement. The irony was exacerbated by the fact that from the late 1970s architects designing houses began to draw their inspiration from the suburban villas hastily erected around cities like Birmingham and London by developers between the two World Wars. Or new housing was derived from turn-of-the-century Arts and Crafts cottages, which were also the model for suburban developers. Architects involved in housing began to investigate vernacular or traditional local building styles as a way of reconciling their profession to their public. In an act of repentance for what now seemed like the sins of the 1960s, many architects subdued their urge to impose formal solutions on housing design and became partners in the process of consulation with local people. 'Community Architecture' led to a spate of kitsch 'Toy Town' housing around British town centres in the 1980s. The architect had descended from Parnassus to the market place.

The speed of construction during the 1950s and 1960s meant that British architects were so busy that there was precious little time to research. Experimental buildings, particularly in the public sector, were erected hastily without the attention to detailing and craftsmanship necessary to make them last. Meanwhile, the art of perspective was neglected. Architecture, through economic necessity, constraints of time and, in part at least, through philosophical choice, had become a process. Systems, diagrams and a rather perverse adherence to the Modernist creed that form follows function, had threatened to turn the typical architect into a cross between a social engineer and scientist.

In hindsight it is not difficult to find the reasons why. The politically led public sector was demanding the construction of hundreds of thousands of cheap new homes a year. These were needed to house both those living in slum conditions and the families that had burst out of the baby boom of the mid-1950s. Prefabrication seemed the obvious answer. The machine age, so many architects justified their approach to design, could and should be able to use its factory system to generate cheap, production-line architecture. The architect's job was to give form and sense to the detailing and grouping of vast estates of new flats and houses. The net result seems less than heroic from the perspective of the present day, when the perils of low-cost prefabrication, the dangers of living in high-rise accommodation and the break up of traditional communities are obvious.

An Architecture of Modesty

To understand how British architecture has become fragmented in the 1980s, it is essential to understand what it had set out to achieve in 1945 and to look at its development over those forty years. The great irony of Modern architecture was that it was meant to be truly popular. It was, after all, an approach to planning and building that was concerned with raising the standard of life for the urban poor and with reconciling the needs of a machine age with human aspirations. In Britain, immediately after the Second World War, some of the very best architecture was the direct result of this social concern.

In 1945, Modern architecture had the best possible start. During the war, Britain had lost upwards of two million houses through enemy bombing. There was a desperate need to build new homes and the success of government-backed, pre-fabricated housing programmes, pursued vigorously between 1946 and 1949, proved that modern industrial techniques and architecture could fuse successfully.

However, great opportunities also arose for political and social reasons. The war years had gone some way to break down class barriers in Britain. Few people, from whatever stratum of society, had escaped the direct effects of war. Apart from bringing British people closer together, the war fostered radical politics. A socialist government was swept to power in 1945. This was partly due to the fact that many voters associated the Conservative party, despite the attractions of Churchill's wartime leadership, with pre-war unemployment and the Depression. The war had also proved that the state was capable of taking drastic, yet responsible, action to ensure that the onus of wartime restrictions fell equally on rich and poor.

Young architects, steeped in Le Corbusier's ideas and a romantic vision of socialism, believed that architecture could start again from scratch, free from the onus of history and precedent. German bombs had already begun to start the process; it was time to rebuild an England without slums, class warfare and the worst effects of the industrial revolution.

Two of the most important factors affecting the early history of post-war architecture were state interference and rationing. During the war years the state had rapidly taken control of areas of production and administration that had previously been run by private enterprise. Within five years of taking office, the Labour government of Clement Attlee (1945-51) had brought Britain's railways, coal mines and health services under state control. National and local government offices expanded with a new generation of administrators. Many of the best young architects then became government employees.

The national and local government initiative in architecture had a dramatic and long-lasting effect. Not until the economic collapse of 1973 did the state show signs of minimizing its role as architectural patron. New housing, new towns, schools, hospitals, libraries, magistrates' courts, fire stations, railway stations, offices for government departments – all these came under bureaucratic patronage.

The early results were popular, successful and critically acclaimed. The unpretentious schools designed by the Hertfordshire County Council Architect's Department under A. W. Cleave-Barr were models of the new democratic architectural spirit. Working with industry, the Hertfordshire architects devised a series of low-cost, prefabricated schools that were light, airy, easy to assemble and unpretentious. The schools were proof that the new architecture could escape the restraints (and possibilities) of any particular style. A shortage of materials encouraged the architects to design minimal structures. When materials became available from the mid-1950s, buildings became increasingly elaborate. These early days of informal architecture were to be short lived.

However, in the short term, the new generation of architects was able to prove that even monumental buildings could be free of historical association, well made and popular. The influential London County Council Architect's Department was responsible for perhaps the best-loved post-war public building, one that has stood the test of time from every point of view. The Royal Festival Hall (completed in 1951, river front remodelled 1962-64; *opposite*) was a wholly Modern building in plan, in form, logic and materials. Yet, far from being rough and ready in feel and appearance, the giant riverside concert hall was dressed in Portland stone panels and fitted inside with smooth, plaster surfaces, delicate lighting and warm, natural materials. It demonstrated a particular pre-war love affair between young British architects and Scandinavian design as much as it evoked the powerful, sculptural forms of Le Corbusier. Sadly, these delightful interiors were later systematically spoilt in the 1980s.

Introduction to Modernism. Royal Festival Hall, 1948-51 (since altered, 1962-64), LCC Architect's Department, under Robert Matthew

Idealistic Modernism. Dunlop Semtex rubber factory, Brynmawr, 1946-49, Architects' Co-Partnership

Perhaps the only other major building of the immediate post-war period to reach the same high standards of design and construction was the Semtex rubber factory in Brynmawr, Ebbw Vale (1946-49; *left*). This vast factory, the work of the Architects' Co-Partnership and engineered by Ove Arup and Partners, was an idealistic attempt to create a workers' palace in the most impossibly run-down area of industrial Britain. In 1939, unemployment in Ebbw Vale had reached 82 per cent. There had been riots there in 1935. Poverty seemed endemic. The new building, a triumph of concrete technology, was lowered down into this depressed area as if from outer space. Like so many truly Modern Movement buildings it was an ideal that owed nothing to the vernacular traditions of the region. It was a temple of industry handed down from Platonic guardians (intellectual, socialist architects in the service of the state) to poverty-stricken casualties of a failed industrial revolution.

15

Festive Modern. Lion and Unicorn
pavilion, Festival of Britain, South
Bank, 1951, R. D. Russell and
Robert Goodden

Festive Modern. Lion and Unicorn pavilion, Festival of Britain, South Bank, 1951, R. D. Russell and Robert Goodden

Sponsored by the Attlee government, the Brynmawr factory – since closed and saved for posterity in 1988 – was a noble failure. The quality of the architecture was never in doubt, but at the time a remote valley in South Wales was not the best spot to build a major rubber factory.

The Royal Festival Hall and the Brynmawr factory are two powerful and intelligent buildings, yet both, in keeping with the post-war utility spirit, were designed by teams who preferred to remain anonymous. The name chosen by the Architects' Co-Partnership emphasized the importance of team, not individual, effort.

Romantic Modernism

However, beneath this puritanical garb, British architects sported colourful undergarments. The British love of the whimsical was evident in the Festival of Britain, a remarkable six-month exhibition of 1951 that filled a bomb site on London's South Bank of the Thames between County Hall and Sir Giles Gilbert Scott's Waterloo Bridge. Under the direction of Sir Hugh Casson (b. 1910), Modern architecture was played out as a hugely enjoyable game for a public anxious for some colour, fun and excitement after years of war, austerity, powdered eggs, prefabs and petrol coupons.

The Festival pavilions (*above*) were glorious examples of stage-set Modern architecture, buildings grouped picturesquely into a Modern Movement funfair. The Festival site was an important essay in picturesque townscape design, an attempt to show that Modern architecture and traditional concepts of town planning were far from incompatible. The Festival pavilions were also the first close encounter the British public enjoyed with Modernism. Although a streak of whimsy and colour might have been just what Modern architecture needed if it were to be popular in Britain, it was not the line that angry young Moderns adopted. If anything, Modern architecture became more severe over the next decade.

Nevertheless, the Festival of Britain spirit was evoked powerfully in the colourful pages of the influential magazine *The Architectural Review* under the editorial direction of Hubert de Cronin Hastings. Casson was a member of Hastings's editorial board, which also included Pevsner. Hastings published Gordon Cullen's visual polemic and guide *Townscape* (1954), which was for many years after an essential primer on picturesque urban planning for British architects. In the meantime, Hastings employed the boisterous and brilliant journalist Ian Nairn to launch his *Outrage* (1955) attack on what he called 'Subtopia', the urban wasteland created after the Second World War by poor land planning and architecture.

The conclusion of this whimsical line of thinking was reached twenty years after the Festival of Britain with the publication of Hastings's *Civilia* (1971), written under the self-mocking pseudonym Ivor de Wofle (*sic*). A collage of Brutalist housing estates, the new universities and new towns massed upon a hilltop site akin to an Italian hill town, *Civilia* was an interesting attempt to blend romantic British notions of the clustered, multi-level Italian town with Modern architecture and services. It suggested that buildings could have a variety of uses, devoid of the dogmatic functional restraints imposed on them by the angry young Moderns, who favoured systems, science and exactitude, and craved for religious certainty.

The New Housing

Lacking a historical base and a well-rehearsed grammar of ornament, Modern architecture could seem lifeless. The new towns designed and built across the country from the end of the Festival of Britain onwards were largely composed of conventional buildings which, while aping Modern forms, were in reality little more than stripped down traditional houses and suburban shopping parades. The only real difference was that the towns were designed around the flow of cars rather than the flow of people.

The fourteen new towns were based on the garden city principles laid down by Sir Ebenezer Howard (1850-1928) at the turn of the century. Nevertheless there was no guarantee that the overall quality of life would be improved by simply lowering the density of an urban population and bringing the city to the countryside. Lacking the amenities and culture of the city, new towns around London, for example, became dormitory suburbs, overspill housing areas for London. Only at Milton Keynes (p. 23), commissioned in 1968, was there a conscious attempt to break new ground.

The quality of new city housing varied enormously. In the hands of inventive, yet socially committed, practices such as Tecton – the practice founded by the Russian émigré Berthold Lubetkin (b. 1901) in 1932

Shock of the New. Cluster Block, Bethnal Green, 1955, Denys Lasdun and Partners

Corbusian Mass Housing. Churchill Gardens estate, Pimlico, 1946-52, Powell and Moya

Sub-Miesian. Hunstanton school, Norfolk, 1949-54, Peter and Alison Smithson

and including Denys Lasdun among its members – local authority estates such as Spa Green in Camden (1949) were planned as rational, elegant additions to the city. It was only when architects began experimenting on people who had no effective say in the design of their houses that estates became the object of extreme hostility. Such a reaction was not aroused by the early, large-scale, post-war estates like Powell and Moya's Pimlico Housing Scheme (now Churchill Gardens; 1946-52; *left*) which still had a delicacy of form, though it is certainly evident in the monumental estates that emerged from the Brutalist thinking of the mid-1950s. The architecture of the late 1940s and early 1950s can almost be described as an architecture of innocence. The unpretentious quality of these buildings make them seem refreshing forty years on.

Angry Young Architecture

The idea that Modern architecture was not only a social duty and process but also a question of ideas and form was given real impetus by Peter Smithson (b. 1923) in his influential lectures in the mid-1950s to students at the Architectural Association. Curiously, Peter and Alison (b. 1928) Smithson had made their name with one of the severest buildings ever intended for human use in Britain. Their school at Hunstanton on the north Norfolk coast (1949-54; *below*) was as 'honest' a building as any Modernist could desire. Its materials were made manifest. Its Miesian logic was relentless. But, in many ways the Hunstanton school summed up the reasons why outright Modernism was never popular in Britain. For a nation of pragmatists, the idea of a building owing everything to an

**Arts and Crafts Updated. Tadley
school, Tadley, 1984-87,
Hampshire County Architect's
Department**

idea – and precious little to the needs of
children and their teachers – was clearly
wrong. Although hugely influential at the
time, Hunstanton was less impressive as a
school than the pragmatic Hertfordshire
schools which were undogmatic responses
to the needs of post-war education.

In Hampshire during the 1980s, the
county architect Colin Stansfield-Smith has
proved that a modern school, such as the
one at Tadley (1984-87; *above*) with its
conical, polychrome roof, can be colourful
and friendly without resorting to Post-
Modern decoration or Neo-Vernacular
whimsy. The gap between Hunstanton and
Tadley is in many ways the story of how
British architecture was transformed so
dramatically over that period.

New Brutalism, as the Smithsons were
happy to label their work, was an
architecture that lived up to its name. The
Park Hill estate in Sheffield (completed
1961), designed by Jack Lynn and Ivor
Smith under the direction of local authority
architect J. L. Womersley, spelt out the
entire Brutalist canon. The rough concrete
finish, adopted from Le Corbusier, was to

become something of a fetish among local
authority architects throughout the 1960s,
culminating in Cumbernauld New Town
and the South Bank complex in London.
Elevated walkways ('deck-access') gave this
vast Modern ship of the urban desert a form
of social congruity; in reality these provided
fast escape routes for muggers and high-
speed racetracks for children on
skateboards and bicycles. The dream,
however, had not been a cynical one
designed to make people's life a misery. In
fact, quite the reverse was true. The estate
was meant to be well serviced with
amenities, while the architectural forms
were intended to be unpretentious, a
positive reflection of the grittiness and
closeness of a working-class lifestyle
romanticized by middle-class professionals
and playwrights.

The rationale governing the design of
estates like Park Hill was set out by the
Smithsons, among other architect members
of what was known as Team X. This group
emerged from the tenth conference of CIAM
(Congrès Internationaux d'Architecture
Moderne), a United Nations of Modern
architecture founded in 1928. The young
architects who dominated the proceedings
of CIAM's tenth conference at Dubrovnik in
1956 believed that early Modernists were
too formal and academic in their approach
to architecture and town planning.
Architects like Gropius and Mies van der
Rohe seemed content to hand down plans
and forms as if from above, rather than to
mould the existing fabric of any given
community into a new form of appropriate
architecture. Park Hill was an attempt to
deduce from local conditions the
appropriate architectural response.

Even so, as with all architectural creeds,
Team X's weighty deliberations resulted
ultimately in just another fashion. The
South Bank complex in London showed the
dire results of playing fashionable games
with such a demanding line of thought.
Intended as a national celebration of the
arts, it has become instead one of the most

Right Concrete landscaping.
National Theatre, South Bank,
1967-77, Denys Lasdun and
Partners

Far right Bombastic Brutalism,
Barbican estate, City of London,
1957-84, Chamberlin, Powell and
Bon

brutal groups of civic buildings erected in post-war Europe. Designed by the Architect's Department of the London County Council and its successor, the now defunct Greater London Council, the South Bank complex comprises the Hayward Gallery (1964-68), a concrete fortress that recalls Rommell's 1944 D-Day defences in Normandy, the Queen Elizabeth Hall (1964) and the Purcell Room (1964) for the performance of orchestral and chamber music. The National Theatre (*above left*), an intricate building of great, if savage, distinction, designed by Sir Denys Lasdun, and the elegant Royal Festival Hall complete this muscular sequence.

If these buildings designed by local authority architects are unpopular, it is because of their raw, humourless character, lack of windows, no obvious entrances and the fact that their rough-cast concrete walls stain markedly in the rain. The connecting walkways drain badly in downpours, while the undercrofts to the complex resemble a sequence of abandoned underground car parks. The architecture of the South Bank had some fans; it became a playground for teenage skateboarders in the late 1970s. In

1987 Terry Farrell (b.1938) was asked to submit plans to redress the exposed spaces and walkways linking the buildings. Farrell's task was to weave these aggressive monuments back into the fabric of the city. This was a particularly difficult undertaking as their rough concrete texture was essentially unsuitable for an urban environment. In devising his *béton brut* (raw concrete) architecture at Unité d'Habitation, Le Corbusier was making a virtue out of necessity. He originally envisaged using steel for the new complex, but, as this was in short supply, he made use of cheap, available concrete worked by inexperienced hands. Set against the backdrop of the craggy mountains beyond, the Unité seems an appropriate monument for its setting. Le Corbusier would have been unlikely to have designed a similar sort of building in Paris. The problem with Brutalist architecture in Britain is that it became an imposed fashion rather than a pragmatic response to a building's site and function.

Brutalism was an angry young architecture belonging to the same period as John Osborne's play *Look Back in Anger*

(1956). The Smithsons and their camp were reacting strongly against the whimsical nature of British architecture stemming from the Festival of Britain. Theirs was also an aggressive response to the gentle approach that led to the Hertfordshire schools. The Smithsons and their followers proposed a return to the heroic architecture of the early Modern Movement, symbolized by Le Corbusier or Mies van der Rohe. It was only a pity that such well-intentioned aggression was channelled into the design of subtopian housing schemes that were meant, in all sincerity, to be utopian.

When finished to a high standard, well maintained and provided with theatres, cinemas, cafés and shops, the elevated housing estate could work, even in raw concrete. The vast, citadel-like Barbican (1957-84; *opposite*), designed by Chamberlin, Powell and Bon for the City of London Corporation, proved popular among professional people with no children. Although stark and abstract, it was well built and imaginatively landscaped with waterfalls, tanked pools and gardens. When the Barbican Centre – a major arts complex – was completed in 1981, and the bars, restaurants and delicatessens long promised finally emerged, the area became a natural home for those with money to spend on the finer things in life.

The Case of James Stirling

However, one of the architects to emerge from the Brutalist camp turned out to be perhaps the most individual post-war British talent. James Stirling (b. 1926), then in partnership with James Gowan, began his independent career with a group of Le Corbusier-inspired brick flats on Ham Common, Richmond, Surrey (1955-58). Stirling's first mature work with Gowan, the Engineering Building at Leicester University (*below*), has been one of the most influential Modern buildings worldwide, since its completion in 1963. The reasons have never

Ad Hoc Modern. Engineering Building, University of Leicester, 1959-63, James Stirling and James Gowan

been hard to see. Wholly uncompromised, it is nevertheless a clever bricolage of some of the key images of truly Modern architecture, mixed with a fond play on the constructional work of the great British engineers of the nineteenth century. Yet Russian Constructivism is the most overt reference in a building that is as much about the process by which it was designed and put together as it is a functioning building. Its clear, diagrammatic programme derived from Stirling and Gowan's technique of using the axonometric as a standard design tool, a way of drawing much emulated from the 1950s onwards. In later years this idea of the building as a machine has been developed by Richard Rogers – notably in the Lloyd's headquarters (1978-86; *below*) in the City of London.

Stirling repeated this approach in the History Faculty Building at Cambridge University (1964-67) and at the Florey Building, a student hostel for Queen's College, Oxford (1966-71). Since its construction the History Faculty has shown many of the same flaws as the Smithsons' Hunstanton school. Hot in summer, cold in winter, and prone to leak, such a building prompted critics to claim that Modern architects were more concerned with style than with construction. Ironically, apologists of Modern architecture had always claimed that Modernism was not a style, but the only true way of building for the twentieth century. As a postscript, the Senate of Cambridge University voted in 1986 on the thorny question of whether to pull down and replace the History Faculty Building. In the end it was repaired; thus an important work of architecture was maintained for posterity.

Pop Architecture

Twenty-five years ago the decision to preserve the Stirling building would hardly have met with the approval of Modern architects. The influential architect and teacher Cedric Price (b. 1931), who designed the Snowdon Aviary at London Zoo (1963; *opposite*), believed that *all* buildings were dispensable. In fact, architecture itself was unnecessary. All that was needed to replace it was a form of servicing that could meet human needs and desires, while liberating mankind from the shackles of fixed forms and frames. Although the practical aspects of Price's work could hardly be realized, his ideas concerning freedom from architectural determinism shaped the way that Pop-influenced young architects of the mid-1960s began to think.

The complex, clever drawings by Peter Cook (b. 1936), Ron Herron (b. 1930) and

High-Tech Gothic. Lloyd's, City of London, 1978-86, Richard Rogers and Partners.

Right Tensile Structure. Aviary, London Zoo, 1963, Cedric Price, Lord Snowdon, Frank Newby

Far right Extruded Modern. Shopping Centre, Milton Keynes, 1976-79, Milton Keynes Development Corporation Architect's Department

Right Tensile Structure. Aviary, London Zoo, 1963, Cedric Price, Lord Snowdon, Frank Newby

Far right Extruded Modern. Shopping Centre, Milton Keynes, 1976-79, Milton Keynes Development Corporation Architect's Department

Michael Webb (b. 1937), three of the architects who formed the experimental group Archigram in 1960, for 'Walking Cities' and 'Plug-in Cities', without following traditional architectural rules, caught the Tune-in, Turn-on and Drop-out, acid-induced philosophy of Timothy Leary and the dreams of boundless freedom evoked in the late novels and Californian lectures of Aldous Huxley. Later, in the 1970s, the idea of a flexible, plug-in architecture was developed by Norman Foster (b. 1935) and Richard Rogers (b. 1933) amongst others. The first monument in this style was the Pompidou Centre in Paris, designed by Richard Rogers and Renzo Piano (b. 1937). Completed in 1977, this vast exercise in Bowellism – the building weaves its insides outside – still has the power to shock ten years later. It has remained as popular as the nearby Eiffel Tower.

The idea of the 'indeterminate building' and the infinitely extendable grid was also taken up in the design of Britain's last major new town, Milton Keynes (1976-79; *above right*), which was to develop continually over the next twenty years. The group of architects working with Derek Walker on its design were much impressed by ideas concerning flexibility and by the infinite grid of Los Angeles, the cult city of the mid-

1960s. Part of the rationale behind Milton Keynes was to create a town that could extend rationally in mixed-use, plug-in blocks, though the attraction also lay in the design of a classless place to live. In fact, the even level of the buildings, coupled to a powerful grid, has made for a town that looks thoroughly new and class-free. Not surprisingly, Japanese and American corporations setting up British offshoots find Milton Keynes a congenial place in which to work.

Concrete and Le Corbusier

The formalist approach to Modern architecture can be seen in the huge programmes that saw the building of Britain's universities throughout the 1960s. Sir Basil Spence (1907-76), who had practised in his early days with Sir Edwin Lutyens, was the most outrageous exponent of mixing architectural metaphors and merging ancient and modern forms. At Sussex University (1964) he was content to play, successfully, with Le Corbusier's Maisons Jaoul. By contrast, Sir Robert Matthew and S. S. Johnson-Marshall used a version of the CLASP method of system building to design a prefabricated campus at York University (1961-64; p. 24). The CLASP system (Consortium of Local Authorities Special Programme) was a way

Above CLASP system. York University, 1961-64, Robert Matthew, S. S. Johnson-Marshall

Right New Formalism. New Hall, Cambridge, 1966, Chamberlin, Powell and Bon

of building in prefabricated panels that brought the Hertfordshire school system up to date in the late 1950s. At York it led to a relatively informal campus, but not one of any great architectural distinction.

At Cambridge and the new University of East Anglia in Norwich, architects like Chamberlin, Powell and Bon (New Hall, Cambridge, 1966; *above*), Powell and Moya (Cripps Building, St John's College, Cambridge, 1967), Ahrends, Burton and Koralek (University College, Dublin, 1971-74) and Denys Lasdun (residential blocks for students at East Anglia University, 1962-68) were experimenting with bold, sculptural, concrete forms. Too often lumped together by a public obsessed with giant housing estates and empty London office towers, the work of the best mainstream architects of the mid-1960s was a collage of images and ideas drawn from such diverse sources as Inca villages and the late houses of Le Corbusier. Perhaps it was the choice of building materials – industrial brick, brute concrete – that made so many of the new buildings unlovable.

As these disparate approaches to Modern architecture reached their most intense phase, the economic crash brought a halt to most work in the public sector. Robin Hood Gardens estate (1968-72; *opposite*) in east London by Peter and Alison Smithson, the most brutal of all those architects' works, represented the last of the great formal experiments in public housing. A rough hewn, concrete sculpture supposedly re-creating the intimacy of the old terraced houses it replaced, along with Erno Goldfinger's Trellick Tower in North Kensington (1968-71), the Robin Hood Gardens estate represented the final flowering of an idealized form of housing that was never loved by those for whom it was intended.

High Tech: the Romance of the Machine

The speed with which architects educated and brought up in a severe, didactic Modern tradition changed course during the 1970s was both remarkable and understandable. In the 1980s, the differences between

Above Streets in the Air. Robin Hood Gardens estate, Bow, 1968-72, Peter and Alison Smithson

Right Structural Rationalism. Cheltenham estate, North Kensington, 1971-73, Erno Goldfinger

architectural styles and schools have become vivid. Nevertheless, there were architects whose work from the 1960s onwards showed an insistent logic and consistent development. Architects who make up this broad Modern church include multi-disciplinary practices embracing architecture, surveying and engineering such as Arup Associates, pragmatic Modernists such as Richard MacCormac (b. 1938) and Edward Cullinan (b. 1938) and experimenters such as Norman Foster and Richard Rogers.

Foster and Rogers set up in practice together as Team 4 in 1967 after post-graduate study at Yale University. Since then, both together and with their own separate practices, they have pursued a theme that pushes Modern architecture along a highly sophisticated technological path, while remaining optimistic about the future and yet full of nostalgia for the heroic days of the industrial age. Crafted, pristine constructions like Foster's Sainsbury Centre for the Visual Arts at East Anglia University (1978; p. 26) and the Hongkong and

Shanghai Bank headquarters (1979-86), stand in splendid isolation from the buildings around them. They maintain the Platonic ideal underpinning the Greek temple and Palladian villa set apart from the mundane world. Although from the mid-1980s, with his projects for the design of a new BBC radio headquarters in Portland Place, London, and the Médiathèque sited opposite the Maison Carrée in the historic centre of Nîmes, Foster has faced up to the question of contextual form, his strength to date has been in designing one-off buildings that have as much in common with a lunar module, aircraft or car as they do with cities, streets, brick and mortar. Like Le Corbusier, Foster is a Romantic Classicist, pursuing an ideal goal.

Richard Rogers's work, however, is closer in spirit to the clip-on, plug-in, 'indeterminate' world of Archigram. In some ways it seems ironical that because of their exposed engineering details and use of expensive materials, High-Tech buildings need to be immaculately hand-crafted not to look crude. Fortunately, both Foster and

High-Tech Classical. Sainsbury Centre for the Visual Arts, University of East Anglia, 1978, Foster Associates

Rogers have been able to command vast budgets to build two of the world's most dramatic and satisfying buildings in the High-Tech genre during the 1980s. Rogers's headquarters for Lloyd's (p. 22) in the City of London cost £168 million, while at something over £800 million, Foster's Hongkong and Shanghai Bank was the most expensive building ever recorded.

Low-cost, High-Tech buildings have continued to sprout across the country in the 1980s, but most have been poor imitations of these two monuments to high finance. Failure of cladding panels and window gaskets has served only to detract from a way of building that requires highly skilled workmen and high-quality materials. Perhaps only Michael Hopkins's Schlumberger Research Laboratories on the outskirts of Cambridge (1985; pp. 152-55 and 157) and his new Mound Stand at Lord's Cricket Ground in London's St John's Wood (1987; pp. 130-32) come close.

An interesting case is the development of the industrial park called Aztec West (pp. 150-151) situated on the edge of Bristol. Unwittingly, this centre for the new breed of computer-based companies has become a prime example of architectural solutions in the 1980s to the simple need to build

attractive, weatherproof, light industrial units. The earliest buildings on the site were shiny High-Tech sheds decorated with structural masts picked out in bright primary colours. Superficially attractive, these buildings suffered from damp and water penetration; High-Tech architecture could not be done on the cheap. Suspicious of architects, the developers then went through a short-lived phase of employing contractors, who both designed and constructed the buildings, which were straightforward but unattractive to the image-conscious businesses the park was hoping to attract. Finally, the developers hit upon John Outram and Campbell Zogolovitch Wilkinson and Gough (CZWG), two practices with very different stylistic approaches, who nevertheless share a common interest in finding materials appropriate for the site. The Post-Modern, Classical sheds of Outram and CZWG prove that a High-Tech business does not necessarily need a building which reflects its activities too literally. At the end of the 1980s the new computer-based industries are working quite happily within membranes of brick, stone, tiles and images drawn from two thousand years of architectural history.

Outrage

On the whole, however, the dominant architectural styles of the late 1970s and the 1980s have been what have been loosely described as 'Post-Modern' and 'Neo-Vernacular'. It is easy enough to understand the return to vernacular forms. In small towns and distant suburbs the visual danger of rectilinear Modern boxes was obvious. Few British market towns escaped from an invasion of bland concrete and brick boxes from the 1960s onwards. Some of these intrusions are considered unforgivable in the 1980s. The Beaufort Hotel, for example, which dominates views of central Bath from Robert Adam's Poulteney Bridge became a casebook example of what Modern architects should not have been allowed to do to old towns, particularly those with a harmonious and, as in the case of Bath, homogeneous urban fabric. Partly as a result of incidents like this, planning permission was refused for large-scale, flat-roofed buildings in unsympathetic materials. The hipped and tiled Mansard roof made its comeback, a time-honoured method of cramming extra storeys into a building without it appearing too tall or overbearing. When coupled with a return to local materials, a rather self-conscious, hackneyed architecture emerged in the early 1970s, designed primarily to slip through local authority procedures with the least friction. Polychrome brickwork, brightly painted planks of wood, rustic ironwork, gables and slate tiles became the clichés of the 1970s. The public had made its complaints about most Modern architecture widely known. Too many architects responded by giving more of the same, except the new shopping complexes, civic centres and housing estates looked as if they had come, jaded, from an all-night, fancy-dress ball.

Very self-consciously, the architectural profession was trying to curry favour with a public that saw it as a menace in the realm of public housing and otherwise in league with ruthless property developers set on a systematic rape of Britain's historic town centres. When the Newcastle City architect John Poulson was jailed for corruption in 1973, the British public felt confident that its instincts were right. This feeling was hardly helped by the most successful commercial architect of the time, Richard Seifert, claiming that he had changed the face of London more than any architect since Christopher Wren. In fact, Wren's buildings were largely restricted to churches rebuilt on their original restrictive sites after the Great Fire of 1666, while Seifert's were, for the most part, speculative office blocks built on historic sites that had been razed to the ground. Although the architect's Centre Point (1962-65) was to receive fresh status

as an icon of Pop architecture in the late 1980s, twenty years earlier it had served as a symbol of the unbridled greed of property speculators encouraged by the Wilson government. Commissioned by the developer Harry Hyams, Centre Point stood empty for many years, the object of public scorn. Ironically, it is a fine building and, despite the jealousy of his rivals, Seifert designed many of the better offices of the time.

The simple fact was that the relatively featureless, straight up-and-down, steel and glass, concrete and glass or stone-clad and glass office tower (whether high-rise or not) was ideal for the purposes of property developers in the 1960s. Imperfect copies of Mies van der Rohe's hugely influential Seagram Building (with Philip Johnson, New York, 1954-58) and Skidmore, Owings and Merrill's Lever Building (New York, 1952-54) shot up on the skylines of British towns.

The Conservation Effect

So, by the time the powerful conservation movement began to exercise its muscles in the 1970s, the British architectural profession was caught on the defensive. It stood accused of ravaging British towns in collusion with property developers and of designing selfish and wilful experiments in public housing. The conservation lobby played on the tendency of most British people to see Modern architecture as a tight-knit, monosyllabic conspiracy. Although this had its propaganda value, it was nevertheless a distortion of history. Modern architecture was never as simplistic as the conservation lobby has led the public to believe. From 1945 onwards, Modern British architecture shifted and twisted in response to changing needs, fashions, materials and ideologies. It was never free from stylemongering. What did exist, however, was an accepted corpus of architectural ideas as well as an abhorrence of decoration for its own sake.

In the short term the success of the conservation lobby lay in preventing further encroachments on city centres. When Geoffrey Rippon, Conservative Secretary of State for the Environment, spot-listed virtually every building in London's historic market site, Covent Garden, in 1979, the conservation lobby had come of age. Until then, there had been drastic plans afoot to raze the entire site to the ground after the closing of the old fruit and vegetable market and its replacement by a banal complex of office towers, international hotels, a giant conference centre (the favourite building type of the 1970s) and other buildings that would have stood better on the fringe of the city. The commercial success of the conserved and revitalized Covent Garden area served to prove that new construction and planning were not the only ways to bring a decaying inner-city area back to life. By the early 1980s it had become taboo to suggest the wholesale redevelopment of a city centre. Architects and developers learnt how to profit from restoration and sensitive 'infill', to stitch the torn fabric of the post-war city back together again. Almost inevitably, urbanism has become the key concern of architects in the 1980s as they have begun working with conservationists and have attempted to please the public.

A Return to Tradition

Much of the silly Neo-Vernacular architecture that emerged from the late 1970s was banal. A loosely related school, labelled 'Romantic Pragmatism' by *The Architectural Review*, achieved considerable critical success at the same time. In work by Richard MacCormac and Edward Cullinan, for example, it was possible to see a reconciliation between traditional materials, craftsmanship and a sense of propriety, and the plans and logic derived from Modernism. This approach to architecture was particularly successful in dealing with the problems of institutional clients such as old established universities and schools, who faced the problem of needing modern buildings types that would not clash with the ancient fabric of the institution. Richard MacCormac's residential building on the lake at Worcester College, Oxford (1983; pp. 120-23) was a handsome example of what could be achieved working in this manner. Buildings of this sort do not fit into an easy category. This is largely because of their highly pragmatic nature. In terms of their response to a brief for a plan first and their unselfconscious exteriors, they are, despite timber or stone cladding, pitched roofs and displays of traditional craftsmanship, some of the most authentically Modern buildings of the 1970s and 1980s.

They are examples of a continuum, a thread that ran through British architecture not just from the Modern Movement, but from the mid-nineteenth century. If their starting point had to be personified, then it could best be found in the Gothic Revivalist, Augustus Welby Pugin. Pugin's great concern was to model the plan of a house not on a formulated principle, as with the ideal Palladian villa, but on strictly empirical and pragmatic grounds. By building walls up from rooms shaped and sized according to their function, Pugin created the essence of the true Modern Movement plan. Yet his buildings abounded with historic reference and traditional craftsmanship.

Monumental Vernacular. Civic offices, London Borough of Hillingdon, Uxbridge, 1973-78, Robert Matthew, Johnson-Marshall and Partners

Modern Classicism. Highpoint II,
Highgate, 1936-38, Berthold
Lubetkin and Tecton

On an everyday level, brick returned as
the dominant building material of the mid-
1970s, replacing concrete. The Hillingdon
Civic Centre (1973-78; *opposite*), designed
by Robert Matthew, Johnson-Marshall and
Partners, was perhaps the single most
important building in the return to brick
and traditional materials.

Less is a Bore: the Post-Modern Influence

This pragmatic approach to architecture
still has a great appeal in Britain and yet the
main style dominating books, magazines
and city centres from the mid-1980s has
been American-influenced Post-
Modernism. While there are no obvious
beginnings to Post-Modern architecture in
Britain, there are a number of pointers.

In 1966, the Philadelphia architect
Robert Venturi published his highly
influential book *Complexity and
Contradiction in Architecture*. The thread
of Venturi's argument was presented in a
series of fast, subjective slogans. 'I am for
messy vitality over obvious unity.' 'I prefer
both-and to either-or.' What Venturi was
arguing for was an architecture of inclusion
that could draw in elements from the
everyday world, the world of mass tourism,
of hamburger stalls, the Las Vegas strip,
Disneyland, Art Deco and Classicism. In
America, Venturi was able to put these ideas
into practice in a repertoire of disparate,
colourful buildings. Twenty-one years after
the publication of his best-known book,
Venturi was invited to design a long-delayed
extension to the National Gallery in
Trafalgar Square. Perhaps because of
difficulties with the planning authorities, the
result was disappointing. In coming to terms
with the messy vitality and contradictions of
London, he seemed to have lost his nerve.

Re-examining History

Modern architects in Britain had long been
playing games with architectural forms.

Many of the best Modern architects were
Classicists at heart, fully in tune with history
but unwilling to ape its forms. Berthold
Lubetkin, whose Highpoint flats at
Highgate (1933-35) were much admired by
Le Corbusier, chose to hold up the entrance
canopy to Highpoint II (1936-38; *above*)
with exact copies of the caryatids borrowed
from the Erechtheum, one of the buildings
that stands on the Acropolis in Athens. For
his contemporary critics, Lubetkin's
decision was seen as a lapse of Modernist
taste, as a move to unnecessary decoration.
But to Lubetkin and to most architects and
commentators in the 1980s, the caryatids
are a delightful reminder of the great
Classical tradition that has woven its way
through Western architecture since the days
of Ancient Greece.

The desire to create a rational order out
of chaos has always been among the first
preoccupations of architects. So it is hardly
surprising to see a Classicial heritage
reworked through the eyes of different
generations. In post-war Britain, this
approach to Classicism can be seen in the
literal tradition of Raymond Erith, Quinlan
Terry and John Simpson, in the Platonic or

Miesian approach of the Smithsons, in the High-Tech temples of Norman Foster, in the colourful abstraction of John Outram or in the Art Deco play of Terry Farrell. It can also be witnessed in the gentle domestic architecture of Jeremy Dixon, and in the folk world of Leon Krier's influential drawings.

Until very recently, British architects were embarrassed to recognize a tradition which most of them thought Modernism had outlawed, and so the first attempts at a Classical revival were very contrived. Stuck-on pediments and painted pilasters were heavy handed, tongue-in-cheek references to the language of Classical architecture, carefully avoiding anything resembling fluency. Imported from the United States, these games were full of wit and irony.

This stick-and-paste approach to architecture seemed at first to comprise the British language of Post-Modern architecture. Terry Farrell made the first move with his lively reworking of a Camden Town garage as the headquarters for the new TV-am company in 1982 (pp. 160-62). Brightly painted and bubbling with Hollywood imagery, TV-am mixed a strait-laced, low-cost approach to office design with playful forms. In later years, Farrell – whose work owes much to that of Michael Graves in the United States – has developed a more inclusive, more formal approach to architecture that has shown itself in large-scale urban renewal schemes at the end of the 1980s. His 1987 design for a large office scheme straddling London Wall in the City of London was a significant step for Post-Modern respectability. As chairman of the Urban Design Group, Farrell was concerned with filling in the 'gaps' in British cities which, he felt, had been insensitively developed in the 1950s, 1960s and 1970s. In Farrell's opinion, new buildings should evoke urban memories and create spaces that people find friendly rather than alienating. Large-scale city buildings should also address themselves to the passer-by on the street. While American architects had

practised this approach since the 1920s, their British counterparts had found it difficult to make large-scale buildings fit happily into city streets.

Although attempts were made throughout the 1950s, 1960s and 1970s to marry Modern architecture with existing cities, the conservation lobby was generally scathing about efforts at what architects called 'Contextualism'. Most conservationists dreamed of a new wave of Georgian buildings, which is what they meant by 'Classical'. Throughout the post-war era, there had been a small number of architects still practising in a Georgian manner. The most distinguished of these was Raymond Erith, whose partner and successor Quinlan Terry (b. 1937) continued the tradition of English Classicism right through the high days of systems analysis, High Tech and Post-Modernism. An exponent of hand-crafted Georgian houses, and later offices and complete town centres, Terry enjoys star status. Trained at the Architectural Association, Terry worked for a spell in the office of Stirling and Gowan before joining Raymond Erith's lonely Suffolk practice. But, in the 1980s, Terry has suddenly been deluged with commissions for confirmed, born-again or New Georgians. What wealthy clients, who have made their fortunes in the City or at the Bar, want are new houses which represent traditional virtues yet avoid the inconveniences of a two-hundred-year-old house.

In fact, houses built in a strictly Modern idiom have been few and far between in the 1980s. For the most part they have been designed as architects' own homes. Notable exceptions include John Outram's polychrome, steel-framed, concrete-clad, Palladian villa (1986; pp. 52-57) for a Swedish entrepreneur in Sussex, Ian Ritchie's High-Tech Eagle Rock House (1983; pp. 60-62) for an orchid collector in a Sussex wood and Richard Horden's Boat House (1982; pp. 40-43 and 45) in Dorset. Quinlan Terry's success, largely brought about by being in the right place at the right time, has guided him into major commercial projects such as the rebuilding of the Richmond-upon-Thames riverside site in a grand and variegated eighteenth-century manner (1984-88; pp. 168 and 170), a speculative office block in Dufours Place, Soho (1984; pp. 68-69), and an unrealized, but hotly contended, proposal for the comprehensive redevelopment of the old Spitalfields Market site on the edge of the City of London (1987). Terry's ascendancy accompanied a return to wood and leather car interiors, hot metal type, a revival of traditional tailoring and the strengthening of Margaret Thatcher's ideologically right-wing government. In 1988 Terry promised to be the Seifert of the 1990s.

The Private Sector

The renascence of an energetic private sector in the British economy has meant that although there is plenty of work in small-scale buildings and interiors for young architects at the end of the 1980s, the wishes of the client have become increasingly important. Unlike young architects working twenty years before on housing schemes in which the client played a minimal role, architects emerging in their own right in the 1980s have had to fight that much harder to sell a design in which they believe. The architecture of this period, apart from exceptional examples such as the Lloyd's headquarters (p. 22) by Richard Rogers and Partners, has been characterized by the art of compromise. The architect is no longer in such complete control of the final form of the building.

The problem of resolving architectural tradition with new building types and new technology has been taken up by other architects working in what can be called a 'Post-Modern framework'. Whether building an industrial warehouse, a pumping station (p. 156) or a country house, John Outram has brought *gravitas* to his buildings. In economic ways, both in

terms of materials and cost, Outram has shown how the Classical tradition can be introduced into contemporary life without becoming too literal. The country house he designed in Wadhurst, Sussex (pp. 52-57), like Stirling and Wilford's Staatsgalerie, weaves together a complex mixture of architectural ideas, myths and references. Although the house is clearly inspired by the Palladian villa and its plan is essentially symmetrical, it makes full use of new technology. An industrial steel frame is covered by panels of colourful, collaged or highly polished concrete. While there is no pretence that this material is anything other than concrete, the way in which the brute material is tamed evokes the rich marble of Imperial Rome or Renaissance Italy.

The interior of the Wadhurst house is a fusion of traditional craftsmanship, seen at its richest in the complex use of veneers and inlays, and modern domestic equipment and technology. Both Modern and Classical, the Outram house is a demonstration in the private realm of how architects can reconcile what have become competing or warring approaches to building, just as Stirling and Wilford's Staatsgalerie has been in the public realm.

The Public Sector

The most obviously successful British example of a reconciliation between architecture and its public, between Modern and historical architecture in the 1980s, has been Stirling and Wilford's Staatsgalerie (p. 32) in Stuttgart. This major art gallery is both landscape and building, a vibrant connection between different parts of the city – at one level the building can be used simply as a passageway – as well as a collage of architectural imagery; Modern, Classical, Pop, are mixed with elements of heroic Modernism. Echoes of the early nineteenth-century, German, Neo-Classical architect Schinkel resound against elements drawn from Le Corbusier. Fragments of part-buried monumental Classical structures are

**Post-Modern Classical.
Staatsgalerie, Stuttgart, 1977-
84, James Stirling and Michael
Wilford**

offset with skin-deep allusions to the nature of contemporary building construction. So what look like massively deep travertine walls are shown to be thin slithers of stone attached to an internal steel frame. Stirling and Wilford show this juxtaposition in a most wilful manner by devising a section of 'broken' wall whereby fallen stones reveal the modern structure behind. Elsewhere – as in the steeply curved cornices of parts of the building – concrete is formed to a perfection normally only achieved with stone.

The interior of the building is a confident mixture of traditional galleries, High-Tech flourishes and nautical imagery. Few British architects had attempted this complex massing and aggregation of architectural ideas, components and imagery. Stirling and Wilford did not always achieve this harmonious mix themselves. It was a difficult, wilful, architectural game, one that pulled together many of the currents in architectural thought and design in the mid-1980s. The Staatsgalerie represents the complexities and contradictions of the Post-

Modern position at its best, although, wisely suspicious of labels, Stirling avoided categorizing it as such.

In the 1960s, Stirling's buildings had fused various strands of Modernist thought concerned with the nature of architecture. In Stuttgart he was able to extend the range of references back to Neo-Classicism and so, by association, to ancient archetypes. To reach this position Stirling went through a fallow period, in terms of actual building, from 1973 to the early 1980s, years in which he taught as Professor of Architecture at Dusseldorf Kunstakademie and worked on schemes integrating Classical elements with the Modern tradition. During this period assistants in his office included the Classical polemicist Leon Krier (b. 1946).

New Perspectives: the Return to Drawing

The lull in architectural activity in the 1970s gave architects the opportunity to reconsider their views as well as to develop drawing skills neglected in the 1960s or again as work picked up in the 1980s. Throughout the 1950s and 1960s, with notable exceptions, drawings skills were whittled to a minimum. Contemporary issues of *The Architectural Review* and *Architectural Design* revealed page after page of diagrams and weasle-thin drawings displaying the bare-bone process of a building under construction. But it was not just a case of architects having too little time to draw. The method and style of drawing which architects chose in the period were both emblematic and necessary ways of designing without complexity, contradiction or decoration. The decline of the architectural perspective was a political act, a choice by the architectural profession at large to deny what it saw as the decadence and immorality of decorative design.

This position was always tenuous, as many of the finest coloured drawings in British architectural history had emerged from great moralists like Pugin and the architects of the Arts and Crafts Movement. The Pop movement brought about the collage, while James Stirling and James Gowan made effective use of the axonometric, *de rigueur* for a younger generation of architects who came to prominence at the end of the 1970s.

In the 1980s, however, architects have begun to employ a rich repertoire of drawing techniques to convey their message. Quinlan Terry uses pen-and-ink drawings and lino cuts to convey the traditional quality and motives behind his Classical buildings. Robert Adam (b. 1948) has begun putting people back into his Classical perspectives, including the architect himself, a Post-Modern gesture that would have been frowned upon in the 1960s (although James Stirling featured in his own drawings in the 1970s), but which today is no different from a Post-Modern author like John Fowles interrupting his own novels to speak to his readers.

Jeremy Dixon (b. 1939) has employed the painter Carl Aubin to convey the idea of a building's enduring qualities (pp. 165-67). Far from Cedric Price's notion of expendability of the early 1960s, Dixon has chosen to have his, as yet unbuilt, projects realized in oils and depicted as they might be after perhaps twenty years of wear and tear. Facing a Jeremy Dixon building, one has no fear that it will show signs of dilapidation within ten years like many buildings dating from the early 1960s. The Dixon paintings also include figures used to show how a space or a building might be used.

Likewise, John Outram has used drawings to reveal the significance of his buildings, to create links between the past and present, myth and reality and to seek the basic archetypes that make up today's office blocks, warehouses or villas.

Architects working in a High-Tech vein – among them Richard Rogers, Norman Foster and Eva Jiricna – use the drawing as a tool, as a means of immediate communication to achieve an end, rather than as an end in itself. For David Connor, the drawing and the building, although connected, exist as distinct entities. Drawn at obtuse angles and peopled with stretched figures (p. 59), they have a life of their own as art-gallery paintings, but still refer to a real building somewhere beyond the canvas.

Learning from the Street

While architects were taking up drawing again, a new force was beginning to make its influence felt on the profession. The moribund state of the British economy during the 1970s was reflected not only in a dearth of high-quality architecture, with notable exceptions, but also in the lack of excitement in the music, fashion and design world. In response to this lethargy Britain produced Punk, a minor revolution in art, fashion, music and urban lifestyle that gradually infiltrated its way into the world of architects and designers like Nigel Coates, Julian Powell-Tuck (b. 1952) and David Connor (b. 1950). This burst of youthful energy was associated with art, craft, fashion and design movements, so that architects working in a genre that has been variously labelled as 'Industrial Baroque' or 'New Wave' created their own sub-culture. In many ways this new wave of architects brought arts, crafts and fashion back into architecture in a way that had been missing since American Art Deco or the British Arts and Crafts Movement.

Perhaps it was curious that a Conservative era should have given rise to some of the most wild and free-spirited design British architecture had seen since the high eclecticism of the 1880s and 1890s, but the new architecture, although energetic and raw, drew on a whimsical tradition that runs through British design in the twentieth century. Powell-Tuck and Connor designed shops for the Punk fashion queen, Vivienne Westwood, in King's Road, Chelsea (1980). Borrowing from Punk, German Expressionist film sets and Russian Constructivist imagery, shops at World's End in Chelsea attracted considerable attention internationally and particularly from the Japanese who took up this Punk Baroque style in earnest in the mid-1980s. In tune with a new generation of young clients who had made their fortunes in fashion, music and broking, Powell-Tuck and Connor have found themselves at the end of the 1980s able to design and build houses (pp. 58-59) to their own specification and then sell on to admirers of their free style.

Meanwhile, at the Architectural Association school in London, Nigel Coates ran his Unit Ten course along Punk-influenced lines from 1978. His NATO group (Narrative Architecture Today) published and converted the idea of linking contemporary street culture with high-minded architectural design to produce a wilful, but well-informed, architecture that found instant appeal with nightclub owners, proprietors of fashionable shops, bars and restaurants. Coates believed, rather like the Archigram group in the 1960s, that the city should not be divided up into strictly functional zones, nor should buildings be inflexible in their use. The spaces between buildings were just as important as the buildings themselves. In short, Coates wanted to see a city connected to all its parts.

Surprised by his own success – he had always believed that he would be teaching and drawing for the rest of his professional career – Coates's unexpected approach to architecture has taken off in the late 1980s with commissions to design the high-profile Metropole restaurant and the popular Caffe Bongo in Tokyo (pp. 85-88). In London he has worked for the fashion designers Jasper Conran and Katharine Hamnett (pp. 142-43). His jewellery shop, Silver (*left*), in Burlington Gardens in Piccadilly (1987) shows his ability to fuse traditional British craft talent with a blend of Festival of Britain whimsy and a well-developed sense of humour. In the Japanese cafés, more outrageous than the shop Silver, components of 1950s jet airliners mingle with 1950s kitsch, stage-set Classicism, new technology and Modernism. In 1988 his practice, Branson Coates Architecture, is designing a multi-functional complex in Tokyo, giving him the first opportunity to construct the type of building with which he believes cities should be provided in the 1980s and beyond.

Coates's contemporaries have also been attracted by the lure of Japan, which by the 1980s has become the most

New Ornamentalism. Silver shop, Piccadilly, 1987, Branson Coates Architecture

Precinct Planning. Paternoster Square, City of London, 1956-67, Lord Holford; Trehearne and Norman, Preston and Preston

fashionable country in young British eyes. This has led to a pragmatic modern architecture that welds traditional and contemporary architectural ideas from both cultures and can be seen in the work of David Chipperfield and Partners, Pawson and Silvestrin, Munkenbeck and Marshall and Rick Mather Architects.

By Royal Command

The greatest compromises of all have been seen, hardly surprisingly, in popular housing. The need for responsive, small-scale housing has been championed throughout the 1980s under the banner of a populist movement known as Community Architecture. The movement has been supported by the Prince of Wales, who has proved to be genuinely interested in architecture and urbanism. The Community Architecture approach has curried little favour with formalist architects. Its adherents, low-church members of the architectural profession, believe in a form of architecture, particularly in the domestic sector, which is overtly responsive to the needs and desires of its users. In other words, architects should not be designing for themselves, but for the people they serve. This aim can best be achieved by architects working within the communities for which they are designing and by consulting users in lengthy open discussions.

Although laudable in intention, the results have often been rather limited and have led to a fresh rash of Toy Town housing in British cities. However, architects like Jeremy Dixon in his schemes at St Mark's Road (pp. 44 and 46-47), North Kensington, Lanark Road, Maida Vale, and in Docklands have shown how popular, low-cost housing can still have a strong architectural form, that housing can be both responsive to users' needs and to imaginative architecture.

The Prince of Wales's pronouncements on the state of British architecture have had considerable political ramifications. They

have also encouraged an accelerating trend towards a new, literal approach to Classicism. The Prince's opening remarks were made during the presentation of the 1984 Royal Gold Medal to the Indian architect Charles Correa at Hampton Court Palace. Addressing the assembled architects, the Prince saw fit to launch an unprecedented attack on the design of Ahrends, Burton and Koralek's scheme for the new National Gallery extension. Referring to their Post-Modern design as 'a carbuncle on the face of an old and much-loved friend', the Prince sunk the practice's chance of winning the commission for the new building in Trafalgar Square. The job was later awarded to Robert Venturi.

In 1987 the Prince again expressed his disapproval of the competition design entries for the redevelopment of the Paternoster site (*above* and p. 171) around St Paul's Cathedral. The winning entry by Arup Associates was concealed from public display for a year while the design was reworked. The Prince was considerably influenced by the Community Architecture groups and by conservationists with Classical leanings. The case of Paternoster Square has been an important development in the architectural and urban design story of the 1980s. Destroyed largely by bombs in the 1940s, the area around St Paul's Cathedral was comprehensively redeveloped in the mid-1950s under the aegis of Lord Holcroft. After much consultation the new stone-clad buildings were arranged in a heavy-handed, formal sequence around Wren's Baroque cathedral. The range of buildings to the west of the site obscured the view of Wren's two-tier portico from Ludgate Circus. The decision to demolish these thirty-year-old buildings in 1987 heralded the rise of new approaches towards urban design. The uncompromising Modernist thoroughfare not far away at London Wall is already being demolished to make way for Terry Farrell's new, Art Deco, Post-Modern towers.

Even so, experience in London in the late 1980s has revealed that comprehensive redevelopment is still possible as long as the site chosen is redundant and not in a prime, historic location. The folly of trying to build anew in a densely packed historic city centre was emphasized in 1985 when the developer Peter Palumbo tried, in a heroic struggle with the City of London and conservationists, to demolish a sequence of late Victorian buildings on the west side of the Mansion House and to replace them with an open piazza dominated by a 1958 design by Mies van der Rohe for an office tower. While there was much sympathy for Palumbo's dedication to an architecture of quality, it was apparent that, politically, he had chosen the wrong site. Undeterred, Palumbo tried again with a choice of two designs by Stirling and Wilford. Again it was the site that undermined his intentions and not the architects' design.

The boom in office building that took place from the mid-1980s was not a blessing for British architects. Responding to the planned deregulation of the Stock Market, which took place in 1986, developers began a year or so before to rush ahead with highly serviced American-style office blocks. The need to build at high speed, but with great care, led developers to choose American architects to design and build this new generation of 'fast-track' office buildings. Well-known American practices like Philip Johnson and John Burgee, Skidmore, Owings and Merrill, I. M. Pei, Cesar Pelli, Kohn Pedersen Fox and Swanke Hayden Connell were courted by developers who felt that British architects lacked the experience and expertise required to design vast steel-framed offices at great speed.

The Vibrant Eighties

The opening up of architecture in the 1980s has caused many older architects and critics to despair. Yet the very richness of architecture in the chaotic 1980s gives real hope that architecture as a public art is becoming popular even if, for the most part, there is a lack of subtlety.

The buildings and interiors included in this book represent the work of some of the most persuasive, if not the most prolific, British talent of the 1980s. Excluded are the profession's leading lights – Rogers, Foster, Stirling among them – as well as many fine architects and competent buildings. Also excluded is the prolific, yet often mediocre, work of most commercial architects. Instead, those architects who are in the vanguard of their profession have been considered; new ways of thinking and working can be seen just as clearly in a small shop interior as they can in a complex office building. What this selection does show is the vibrancy of the British architectural scene in the 1980s and the hope that offers for the future, especially now that architects, developers, princes, conservationists, and even politicians, are beginning to work together.

Houses

New public housing has all but disappeared in the 1980s. New, low-rental developments have been left mostly in the hands of housing associations recruiting architects to work on the conversion of old city dwellings. Throughout the decade the Conservative government has encouraged council tenants to buy their homes. The Thatcher ideal has been one of a nation of enterprising, share-owning, home-owning new Victorians.

Some of the most significant achievements in the public realm have been those brought about by Jeremy Dixon at Lanark Road (1982) and St Mark's Road (1975-80; pp. 44 and 46-47) in north west London. Clearly belonging to their times, both groups of housing demonstrate how architects can design humanely and imaginatively while fitting their buildings into existing street patterns. The problem of much housing before the 1980s was its overtly experimental nature. The only unabashed Modern scheme to meet with some degree of critical approval was the Maiden Lane low-rise estate on the edge of Hampstead Heath designed by Benson and Forsyth (1981). It was hailed by *The Architectural Review* in 1983 as 'representing the very best in British housing'. Some of the most expensive council homes ever built and requiring constant care, Maiden Lane owed an unembarrassed debt to Le Corbusier. Yet only five years later a report prepared for the London Borough of Camden found that 'the breakdown at Maiden Lane is complete. The community is at odds with itself [and] with the buildings it inhabits . . . Conditions on the estate are seen by the police as being a time bomb for the future.'

The boom area, however, has been in highly serviced, luxury flats near city centres. The deregulation of the London Stock Market in 1986 encouraged developers to convert old Dockland warehouses into fashionable flats and eventually to build new, luxurious, high-rise blocks. One of the most dramatic was Michael Baumgarten (b. 1950) and Rick

Mather's redevelopment of the grim, early 1960s West London Air Terminal into Point West, a Manhattan-style condominium. When local authorities sold off their unpopular tower blocks to private developers they found ready buyers, proving as had been suspected all along, that there is nothing inherently wrong with high-rise architecture, but that twenty-storey blocks need proper maintenance and are unsuitable for families.

Much effort over the decade has gone into the rehabilitation of earlier housing schemes, with both private developers and local authorities keen to improve property that had reached its nadir. Hunt Thompson Associates' renovation of Paradise House in Hackney (1985), a 1930s block of streamlined, brick council flats, showed how simple replanning of old courtyard estates, which brought residents their own front doors and gardens, could give a completely new lease of life even to what were called 'sink' estates – those which were inhabited by families on local authority books who could sink no lower. Hunt Thompson Associates kept an office on site while the work was in progress to maintain a continual dialogue with residents, a practice rarely carried out in the 1960s. However, not all 'Community Architecture' has been of this calibre. At its best, for example in Ralph Erskine's estate at Byker, Newcastle (1976-81), the campaign against what many Community Architects saw as the arrogance of their own profession could lead to buildings of aesthetic as well as social quality. Too often, however, the net effect of Community Architecture has been a rash of folksy cottages.

In the private realm, there have been few distinctly modern houses of consequence, partly because of a change in taste among those able to commission new buildings. A return to traditional values has prompted a revival of Classicism. In the late 1980s Classical villas in an eighteenth-century idiom have become fashionable among clients wanting the trappings of Georgian life without the draughts, bowing walls and other inconveniences that form a part of most two-hundred-year-old buildings. Quinlan Terry has built several Georgian-style houses in traditional materials for bankers, brokers, barristers and politicians. Terry's work in the 1980s has ranged from a summer house for Michael Heseltine in Oxfordshire to the design of six new villas in Regent's Park. Rather like the eighteenth-century follies and temples at Stowe, these appear in various styles: Gothic, Doric, Ionic and so on.

Julian Harrop (b. 1945) was commissioned to design a chaste and correctly proportioned Villa Rotunda (1983-84) for the Ferranti family in Cheshire. Not a traditional architect by training or practice, Harrop used computers to help in the design of the late twentieth-century Georgian house. John Simpson (b. 1954) has built a new four-square house in Ashfold, Sussex (1986-89) based on the work of Sir John Soane (1753-1837), while the appropriately named Robert Adam has attempted to break new boundaries by creating what are essentially Georgian

houses, yet making use of contemporary techniques, materials and components.

Although well built, these new Georgian houses are often designed in a way which is quite inappropriate for their scale. Packed with incident they seem, for the main part, fussy, rather like giant doll's houses, and lack the simple grace of equivalent-sized houses built in the eighteenth century.

The Palladian villa has begun to exercise a fresh fascination on architects. John Outram's re-creation in modern materials at Wadhurst in Sussex (pp. 52-57) is an altogether more interesting attempt to fuse the best elements of eighteenth-century landscaping, proportion, planning and craftsmanship with a modern sensibility.

Perhaps the most distinguished houses built in a Modern idiom are the Eagle Rock House (pp. 60-62) designed by Ian Ritchie (b. 1947), which resembles a petrified aeroplane found in a forest clearing, and the Boat House (pp. 40-43 and 45) by Richard Horden (b. 1944), which reaffirms faith in new materials and sweeping modern interiors.

Boat House, Poole, Dorset

Richard Horden Associates

The Boat House (1982) is one of the most convincing essays in prefabricated industrial house design. The idea of the prefabricated house assembled from industrial components and eliminating the use of 'wet trades' (concrete mixing and brick laying) was an early ideal of Modern Movement architects. However, when British architects used mass production methods to build new public housing quickly after the Second World War, the results were all too often ugly, expensive and little loved.

Horden's house in contrast is an exquisitely hand-crafted 'one-off', a building that could have landed from outer space. A keen yachtsman, Horden made extensive use of standard yacht components in the construction of this house. Horden has followed the precedent established by Charles and Ray Eames in their influential, industrial-look house at Santa Monica, California (1949) and more recently by Michael Hopkins in Hampstead, London (1975) by using materials (steel, aluminium, neoprene) well suited to the industrial process. Built in 1982 on a five-by-four modular grid, the Boat House is akin to a giant Meccano model. Its logic is as satisfying as it is relentless.

Above Details of blinds

Opposite House abounds with details drawn from boat technology

Overleaf Made entirely from prefabricated sections, the Boat House is meant as a prototype rather than a one-off

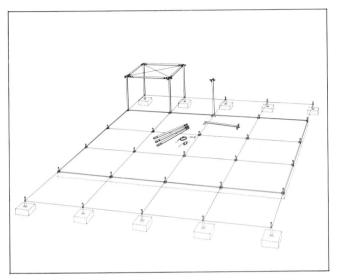

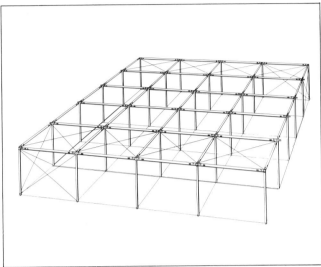

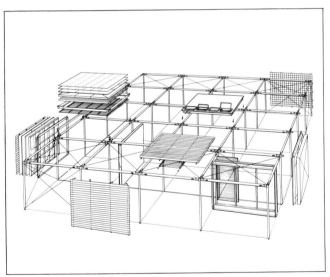

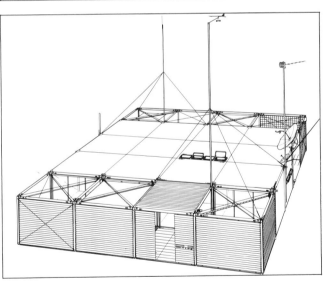

Top left Basic components and grid of Horden house

Top right Complete structure

Bottom left Roof and wall cladding systems

Opposite Dutch-influenced façade of St Mark's Road

Bottom right House complete with aerials and masts

St Mark's Road, North Kensington, London

Jeremy and Fenella Dixon

**Houses march along the street in
step with tradition**

Architects reacted to the unpopularity of giant, mass-produced, featureless urban housing blocks by turning their backs on Modernism and plundering the architectural vocabulary of Enid Blyton's Toy Town. A few adhered zealously to Modernist values and dug a grave for themselves. Jeremy Dixon found his own footing and has designed several housing schemes in London for both the public and private sector that marry traditional and Modern thinking. Although his work has moved increasingly towards the Classical, this rental housing scheme (1975-80) in North Kensington has been designed in a style very much of Dixon's invention. Combining Dutch gables, references to De Stijl and the street sense of traditional London housing, Dixon has created a colourful and popular housing type that is also thoughtful and worth repeating. Most importantly, Dixon re-created a historic and understandable streetscape. The houses in St Mark's Road *belong*, particularly with their steps up to the doors, pyramid-topped gateposts and jutting bays, all of which are elements and devices common to the way we see and imagine London streets.

Historical and modern motifs combined in Dixon's façades

David Wild house, Camden Town, London

David Wild

David Wild's house, built by the architect for his own use and completed in 1985, is remarkable for its commitment to an approach to Modern urban housing that has been all but abandoned in the 1980s. Wild's house is uncompromisingly Modern. Yet it is also clear proof that Modernism can be a part of our vernacular tradition. The Wild house is very much a part of the Camden Town street it adorns, a rational design that eschews the rough concrete finishes of urban housing of twenty years ago. The concrete finish is pristine and the elegantly restrained, yet inventive, façade a rebuke to the rash of Toy Town housing that has disfigured British cities over the past decade. With its elegant, light and sophisticated interiors, its neat provision for parking, its roof terrace and commodious accommodation packed into a tight space, Wild's house shows that in denouncing all things Modern, the British have thrown out the baby with the bathwater. Against the odds Wild has nurtured a distinctly Modern house that could have provided a model for mass housing. Sadly it has in some ways come twenty years too late.

Above Filtered sunlight of modern icons

Opposite Entrance and car port

Opposite Library and roof structure

Above Geometrical abstracts: the kitchen

Far left Light filters through to all levels of the house: detail of stairwell

Left The influence of Mondrian and the Bauhaus: detail of stairwell

The New House, Wadhurst, Sussex

John Outram Associates

New wealth generated in Mrs Thatcher's 'enterprise Britain' has led to a spate of new country houses, most of which have been designed in a Classical idiom. This remarkable steel-framed, concrete-clad, Neo-Palladian villa (1986) is the exception. 'Our architecture', says John Outram of his practice's exuberant work, 'takes Classicism for a walk.' In this case, a walk in a rolling Sussex deer park. Certainly the approach that Outram, perhaps Britain's most inventive and articulate architect, takes to Classicism is a breath of fresh air. It is never literal. The house boasts a Classical plan complete with enfilade along the garden front and the crafted, jewel-box interiors share all the richness of an equivalent eighteenth-century villa. It sits in perfect harmony with the old landscape. The polychrome, terrazzo-like concrete walls are wholly new in spirit, as are the bent plywood vaults over the principal rooms. Visitors are faced with a mysterious windowless front on arrival, but once through the rich, tomb-like hall they are given generous views of the valley beyond, visible through a continuous sequence of wall-to-floor windows.

Above Polychrome concrete columns support glazed walls on garden front

Opposite Sepulchral entrance hall

Overleaf Garden terrace with remodelled conservatory on the far left

Opposite Outram's architectural palette – from brick to 'Blitzcrete'

Top Enfilade looking from the library; ceiling vaults in bent plywood

Above left Modern Classicism: vaulted dining-room overlooking gardens

Above right Cross axis looking towards conservatory past trellis-work doors

Arrow House, Napa Valley, California

Powell-Tuck, Connor and Orefelt

The Arrow House (1984-88) could be considered one of the first Deconstructivist domestic landscapes. In other words, the architects have, in this dramatically angled house, taken apart key radical twentieth-century architectural styles and put them back together into a convincing, if theatrical, whole. The garden is part of that whole. Yet despite its remarkable appearance, the Arrow House is built strictly from local materials (Californian redwood rendered in stucco) and by local craft skills. The centre of a working vineyard, the Arrow House can be seen as a Palladian villa, although its proportions do not follow a mathematical rhythm. A complex pattern of angles, the design does impose certain limitations on living space. The prognathous master bedroom, for example, juts out from an upper floor, its walls meeting at an acute angle that limits usable space inside. Originally the house was to be far more extreme, a theatre if not of domestic cruelty, then certainly of architectural adventure at the expense of domestic routine.

Opposite **North face of free-standing guest wing**

Top **Heavily protected south face; entrance under angled gateway**

Right **Imaginary view of guest wing. Drawing by David Connor**

Far right **Guest tower, pool and landscaping as originally proposed. Drawing by David Connor**

Eagle Rock House, Uckfield, Sussex

Ian Ritchie Architects

Eagle Rock House (1983) by Ian Ritchie recalls the fossilized air frames of forgotten bombers found occasionally in Pacific island jungles. Designed for an elderly collector of rare orchids, the house hides in the undergrowth of a rural Sussex demesne. Climbing frames placed in front of the steel and glass walls of this skeletal, single-storey High-Tech house will ensure that, as nature takes hold, Ritchie's vision will disappear under the advancing foliage. Ritchie has worked for Norman Foster, although his approach to High-Tech design is decidedly more Gothic than Foster's cool Classicism. Assembled from steel frames, struts, rods and wires, Eagle Rock House appears to have been fabricated from a bumper box of Meccano.

Its peripatetic owner asked Ritchie for a 'packing case' rather than a conventional house. The house does look as if it could be folded into a container for easy transportation. Ritchie's design is based around a long fuselage crossed at the centre by a pair of wings. The nose of the fuselage is an elaborate *porte-cochère* which leads through the double-height living space and on into a raised conservatory in the tail. The wings flap over guest accommodation on one side and the owner's private suite on the other. Light, airy, cheap and easy to build, the house on Eagle Rock is a clear demonstration of how an imaginative client can give full creative flight to the architect's imagination without breaking the bank.

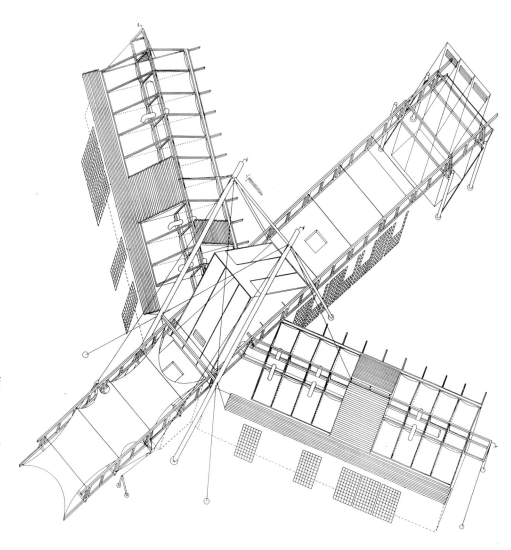

Above Axonometric drawing of Eagle Rock House: entrance left; conservatory right

Opposite Wing, showing blinds for sun protection and trellises for fast-growing plants

**Detail of mast structure
supporting body of house**

Offices

Big Bang was the sonorous name given to the deregulation of the London Stock Market, an event which took place in October 1986. In freeing the City of London from age-old restrictive practices, stockbroking became the fiercely competitive business it had always looked from the outside. The effect on British architecture was immediate, long lasting and revolutionary. Big Bang led to an urgent new demand for office space in the City. Not only were new buildings needed rapidly, but they also had to make space for the new computer technology as well as to act as showpieces for major international banks and trading houses.

The need for a sophisticated new breed of City offices had been foreseen by developers. Among the first to act were Stuart Lipton and Godfrey Bradman of Rosehaugh Stanhope. The first of these buildings was 1 Finsbury Avenue designed by Arup Associates (1984; pp. 72-75). A vast, High-Tech, glass-covered courtyard reminiscent of Decimus Burton's Temperate House at Kew Gardens (1861), 1 Finsbury Avenue won design awards and brought a handsome return to its developer. But, when Lipton invited Arup Associates to complete the design of his colossal, fourteen-phase Broadgate development on the site of Broad Street and Liverpool Street stations on the fringe of the City of London (p. 179), Arup Associates politely turned him down. Unwilling to take on many new architects who would have upset the balance of this finely tuned, multi-disciplinary practice, Arup Associates saw the major part of the significant office and retail development pass to the New York and Chicago practice, Skidmore, Owings and Merrill (SOM).

American practices have begun to move on to the British stage in force. SOM have not only been commissioned to design Brobdingnagian, Post-Modern office blocks at Broadgate, but they have also been charged with the master plan of Canary Wharf (p. 178), the vast development in the north of the Isle of Dogs in London's Docklands. SOM have been joined by the New York practices of Kohn Pedersen Fox, Cesar Pelli and I. M. Pei at Canary Wharf, the site chosen by the American developer G. Ware Travelstead for three 850-foot office towers (the tallest in Europe) to punctuate a mass of low-rise office, retail and leisure buildings. Travelstead later pulled out of the venture, selling it to the Canadian developers Olympia and York.

Meanwhile John Burgee Architects with Philip Johnson (b. 1906), one of the pioneers of European-influenced International Style architecture in the United States, were commissioned, in 1986, to design London Bridge City Two, offices stretching along the South Bank of the Thames between London and Tower bridges. Johnson chose to play a Post-Modern game and design the buildings in the style of Barry and Pugin's Palace of Westminster (1836-52). Construction of this steel and glass Gothic monolith was delayed after opposition from the local authority and by new designs by, among others, John Simpson in 1989.

Other American practices, Swanke Hayden Connell and Heery Associates among them, have opened London offices and fitted their work into the framework of British architecture. The Americans have been successful because developers feel that they possess talents and expertise lacking in their British rivals. Principal among these is their long experience of both steel-framed office buildings and fast-track construction techniques. The 'fast-track' process means that the design and construction of a building concur. Traditionally, British architects would design a building in its entirety before construction.

Office buildings of the 1980s have changed considerably in nature from those of the 1960s. The slim skyscraper block, exemplified by Seifert's Centre Point, or the offices forming the American-style heart of Croydon in Surrey were outdated twenty years after construction. In the 1980s, the sheer range of technical and electronic services has meant that offices require deep-floor plans and high floor-to-ceiling heights to accommodate raised computer floors and suspended service ceilings. The office of the 1980s has also been typified by an 'atrium' or courtyard (technically speaking an atrium is open to the sky) which brings daylight into the heart of deep-plan offices.

Although there has been much talk during the decade about the shift from working in offices to working from home, the office boom of the 1980s has refuted this theory. While it is true that attitudes to the place of work have become more flexible in Britain during the 1980s, people still seem to prefer to carry out business in an office.

Throughout the decade existing office buildings have continually been refurbished and remodelled. John Outram successfully clad two early 1960s examples for Harp Central Heating in Swanley, Kent (1984). What looked like Roman temples of power, complete with stylized flames reaching out from the capitals of the columns, in fact consisted of a concrete- and steel-framed structure of twenty years earlier rescued from the ravages of excessive heat gain in the summer and equally excessive heat loss in the winter.

The new Lloyd's headquarters (1978-86; p. 22) designed by Richard Rogers and Partners and the Hongkong Shanghai Bank (1979-86) by Foster Associates prove that offices can be transformed into buildings as impressive and memorable as New York's Chrysler (1930) and Empire State (1931).

Office influenced by us

Civic centre, Chester-le-Street, County Durham

Faulkner-Brown, Watkinson, Hendy and Stonor

The 1980s equivalent of a Victorian town hall, the civic offices in Chester-le-Street (1983) represent a well-established and familiar building type in a new, overtly High-Tech guise. Even so, the architects have adopted some familiar devices from this glistening building's nineteenth-century forebears. Like any real town hall, the building is centred around a tall clock tower, while much of the imagery is drawn from distant echoes of heroic nineteenth-century industry. However, along with the architectural language, the plan is conspicuously different from earlier town halls. The whole point of the building is public accessibility. As a result, the plan revolves around a light and airy central street that channels a sloping path down through the building. Inside there is a public restaurant, bar and waiting area, all stretched out generously on a bed of Astroturf, which makes this one of the most civilized suites of civic offices in Britain. The building presents a slick surface to the street. The interior, however, is dominated by giant, brightly coloured servicing ducts: it is the Bowellist approach to architectural design popularized by Richard Rogers. Above all the interior is informal and is entirely free from traditional symbols of civic pomp or authority. The colours are bright, the floor covered in modishly studded rubber, while vegetation sprouts in abundance.

Above Street running through building links parallel streets: roof is High-Tech equivalent of Gothic vaulting

Opposite Civic monument updated: municipal clock tower

Dufours Place, Soho, London

Erith and Terry

Rather like the zealous Gothic Revivalist A.W. Pugin, Quinlan Terry believes there is only one correct form of architecture. While Pugin branded Classical architecture as pagan and therefore wrong for a Christian society, Terry believes that God handed down the canons of Classical architecture on stone tablets from Mount Sinai. Classicism is therefore religion as much as architecture. Both architects agree on one point; their adopted style is the only valid one and all buildings can be designed in the same idiom. This lofty block of speculative offices and flats in London (1984) was Quinlan Terry's first significant intrusion into urban design. A severe and simple architectural solution to a straightforward brief, the building at Dufours Place is nevertheless animated with Terry's Mannerist posturing. The exaggerated, if not quite playful, perspective of the door and window surrounds are a case in point, as are the delicate scrolled gables and tall, thin lantern. Stripped of these sweet conceits, the block has more in common with the Classicism of the 1930s than the 1730s, although it is none the worse for that. More important perhaps is that Dufours Place marks a significant attempt by a developer to avoid crass Modernist themes, which by the 1980s had become devoid of any meaning whatsoever. As if doing battle, Terry's lofty brick façade with stone dressing faces one of the blandest 1960s blocks in the area.

Top Optical trick: detail of main entrance

Above left Strait-laced street front highlighted with mannerist flourishes

Above middle Modern Classicism: eighteenth-century meets modern fire regulations

Above right Detail of cupola and service ducts

Opposite Approach from Marshall Street

Starckmann office, Marylebone, London

Pawson Silvestrin

Evidently appropriate for art galleries, houses and restaurants, Pawson Silvestrin's stark Minimalism does not at first appear the obvious style in which to design an office. However, in 1988 the architects were commissioned to design an office and distribution centre for the academic book wholesaler Bernhard Starckmann. The only additions made to the scene in the photographs are one or two desks and several neat stacks of books. Housed in an old milk depot immediately to the north of London's Marylebone Road, the Starckmann office is an essay in absolute Minimalism. The architects spent their client's money on well-crafted and subtle finishes rather than thinly spread decoration and conventional office fittings. The various offices are segregated by delicate screens and by changes in level. Typically the walls are finished in white and the floors in varnished beech. The atmosphere created with the sun shining on the white walls is remarkably calm. Like the architects' Wakaba restaurant, this low-cost office breaks all the accepted rules.

Above Walls and partitions are painted in white

Right Distinctive partition between offices

Opposite View along first-floor offices

1 Finsbury Avenue, City of London

Arup Associates

1 Finsbury Avenue (1984) has been much praised for raising the standard of speculatively designed office buildings. What largely distinguishes the building is its plan. Based around a closed internal courtyard, the offices also look on to the surrounding City streets. The courtyard has been elegantly designed and fitted out to a high standard. Far above the floor is a fretwork of steel roofing that owes its origin to buildings such as the mid-Victorian iron and glass Temperate House at Kew Gardens. A throwback to the commercial *palazzi* of the Italian Renaissance, such covered courtyards (or atria) have become an essential ingredient of office buildings with any pretence to sophistication in the 1980s. The floor-to-ceiling heights of 1 Finsbury Avenue are noticeably greater than those of its predecessors. The extra room was required for raised floors to cover computer and telecommunications cabling and wiring as well as for suspended ceilings containing recessed lighting and air-conditioning plant. A stern building, 1 Finsbury Avenue nevertheless displays a certain flamboyance with its dramatic courtyard roof and its sequence of steel struts and braces that further echo the architects' passion for the great engineer-designed structures of the high-Victorian era.

Above Offices grouped around internal glazed courtyard bringing daylight to all users

Opposite Palm-house roof to atrium

Overleaf Machine-like grid of 1 Finsbury Avenue façade

Carroll, Dempsey

Brownlow Mews, Clerkenwell, London

David Chipperfield and Partners

This advertising agency office in Clerkenwell was designed in 1986. Its architect David Chipperfield, one of a successful new wave of British architects returning to the certainties and possibilities of early Modernism, would not be insulted if the claim was made that it was designed in Paris in 1926. Chipperfield has been a confirmed Modernist since his student days at the Architectural Association. He wrote his thesis on Le Corbusier, but claims to be more concerned with the pragmatic aspect of architecture rather than the idealistic. The contemporary architects he most admires are European Rationalists like Alvaro Siza, Luigi Snozzi and José Rafael Moneo as well as Japanese Minimalists such as Tadao Ando.

Brownlow Mews is an early example of Chipperfield's pragmatic Modernism, a straightforward, crisp white interior making sparing use of colour and placing formal emphasis on a few key points in this converted warehouse building. Unlike Modernists of sixty years ago, Chipperfield does not believe that Modernism has some special hold on morality, nor that it is the only way in which to build.

Opposite **Entrance hall and stairs**

Above **Reception area**

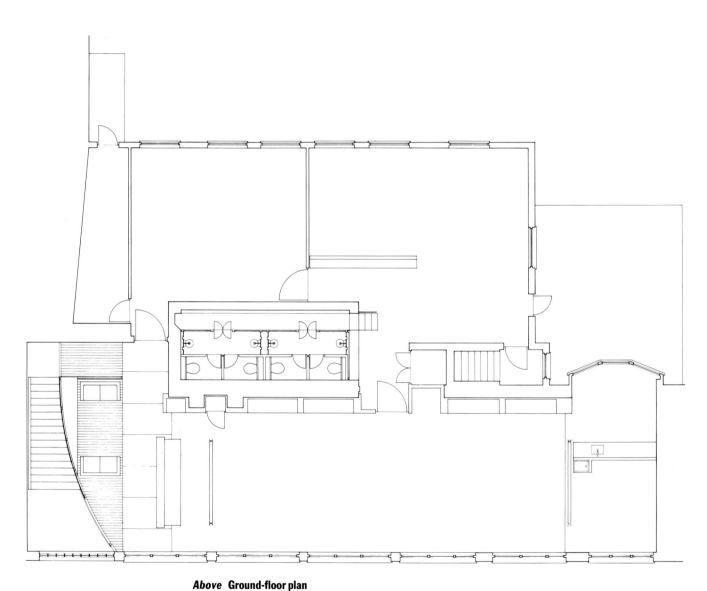

Above Ground-floor plan

Opposite High-level stairs and passageway

Queen Street, City of London

Terry Farrell Partnership

This office block at Queen Street in the City of London (1986) is one of Terry Farrell's more restrained buildings. A straightforward office development in terms of plan and accommodation, it is nevertheless important in the way that it addresses the street in which it is situated. This is a well-mannered building, fitting neatly into its context despite borrowing from Manhattan and Viennese sources. The Manhattan influence is witnessed in the way the building climbs up from the pavement, beginning with a highly polished and richly modelled base through a straightforward central section, which can be seen as an extended *piano nobile*, and ending in a highly articulated roofscape. This was the classic model adopted by the designers of the great Art Deco skyscrapers in New York but the same theme works well in London, as this building proves. The Viennese link is seen in the façade, particularly in the base, which borrows its detailing from the great Secessionist architect, and one of Farrell's heroes, Otto Wagner (1841-1918). Despite its eclectic influences, the building is unpretentious. The detailing of the façade makes it clear that the exterior panels have been clipped on and are not solid marble or granite.

Top left **Zoned roofscape**

Top right **Corner detail adapted from Otto Wagner**

Right **Drawing showing the way the architect has massed the building**

Restaurants, Cafés, Bars

Until the 1980s British cities were starved of the kind of restaurants, cafés and bars that have always made travelling to the Continent so refreshing. The place to find cheap, decent British cooking, it is still said, is at home. Continental-style bars, cafés and modest restaurants have hardly been encouraged by Britain's bizarre licensing laws (revoked in Scotland and slowly changing in the rest of the United Kingdom).

Since the 1980s this position has begun to change and in its wake has come a boom in European-style bars and cafés. The increase in consumer spending, the craze for faddish foods and the rise in the number of single people and childless couples with high disposable incomes have encouraged the construction of new places to eat and drink. The upsurge in the number of professional women has also been a powerful incentive for change. Many women, together with an increasing number of men, find traditional city pubs are not congenial enough to enter for lunch-time or evening refreshment and have thus created a demand for new places to eat and drink.

London is the centre of this feverish activity. Many young architects and designers are able to establish or bolster reputations with designs for cafés and bars. The preserve of interior decorators until the 1980s, restaurants have become the focus for architectural experimentation. Architect-designed restaurants range from cool High Tech and Minimalist interiors to the outlandish Industrial Baroque of Nigel Coates (pp. 85-88) who designed three restaurants in Tokyo between 1985 and 1988.

The first noticeable architect-designed bar was Zanzibar in London's Covent Garden (1976; p. 106) by Julyan Wickham (b. 1942). A haunt for the literary and media Mafia, Zanzibar is distinguished by Wickham's long, snaking bar which allows drinkers anywhere along its length to acknowledge distant cronies. Unlike the traditional British pub which is designed with the privacy of the drinker in mind (with

screens to conceal the identity of the drinker from bar staff, plenty of corners to hide in, and a labyrinth of small bars in which to form private groups), Zanzibar is concerned with public display.

Wickham's City restaurants for the wine merchants Corney and Barrow (1983; pp. 100-01) have developed the theme, while Tchaik Chassay's Groucho Club (1984) in London's Soho is the apotheosis of the bar-brasserie as a place to 'see and be seen'. Chassay took the idea of the traditional club interior and brought it up to date with a dash of Manhattan for a membership of film-makers, journalists and publishers.

The idea of the restaurant and bar as stage has caught on quickly. The sets have largely been designed by architects. Eva Jiricna's Joe's Café (1985; pp. 92-94) for the fashion designer Joseph Ettedgui in London's Brompton Cross made High Tech chic. A style that had been passed down from the great Victorian engineers' bridges, exhibition halls and railway stations was now deemed appropriate for one of the capital's most fashionable lunch-time meeting-places. Jiricna's Le Caprice (1981) behind the Ritz Hotel became another favourite spot for wealthy trendsetters. Big, open and noisy, brasseries have only recently become popular in Britain and bridge the gap between bars and restaurants. Julyan Wickham's Notting Hill Gate brasserie, Kensington Place, in west London (1988; pp. 102-04) sets a trend for this new type of meeting-place. This brasserie is also significant in that the architect had a free hand in the design of not simply the plan and décor, but also the light fittings, tables and chairs.

Ethnic restaurants have changed considerably during the 1980s. The typecast, cheap Chinese and Indian restaurants with their kitsch, flock-paper décor and 'downmarket' image have gradually given way to restaurants that are as glamorous as their Italian and French counterparts. Rick Mather's Zen W3 in Hampstead (1985; p. 84) and Zen Central in Mayfair (1987) blended sophisticated Chinese cuisine with restrained white, modern interiors. Touches of glamour have been added, in Zen W3 for example, by water flowing down the banister of the stairwell.

The fashion for Minimalist restaurants has been set by the new generation of Japanese restaurants with their sushi bars and kitchens on display. The most extreme and satisfying of these is John Pawson and Claudio Silvestrin's Wakaba (1987; pp. 89-91) in London. Scrubbed oak tables, natural materials and a complete absence of decoration concentrate the mind and stomach on the delicate and decorative food.

Outside London the 'theme' restaurant and pubs have kept architects and designers busy dreaming up banal ways of selling banal food. Of the fast turnover chain restaurants, one of the most adventurous is Pizza Express which commissioned Thompstone, Wintersgill, Faulkner to devise a new image for this well-established and popular Italian fast-food outlet. The practice's spacious, white modern restaurant on Lavender Hill, Clapham (1985) is something of a landmark in the design of fast-food chains.

Zen W3, Hampstead, London

Rick Mather Architects

Zen W3 (1985) was very probably the first Chinese restaurant in Britain to steer away from hackneyed ethnic décor. Though a number of raw, functional interiors are to be found elsewhere, none have the undisputed elegance, lightness and clarity of Rick Mather's Zen W3, the first, to date, in a chain of three restaurants. Food in all of the Zen restaurants is light, clean and crisp. The architecture matches the menu. Mather has organized the Hampstead restaurant on two floors around a central atrium. The gallery is reached by a staircase, the banister of which has been transformed into a cascade of water which gurgles agreeably, setting the tone of a particularly gentle ambience. The colours, surfaces and furniture are all classic Modern. This is one of those interiors that has achieved a delicate balance between its design and its function. Change any one element, add an unnecessary colour or picture, and the design would be thoroughly spoilt.

Above View from entrance.
Upper floor reached via waterfall
staircase

Opposite Bar: ancient Rome
meets London street fashion in
Caffe Bongo

Overleaf Aeroplane wing cuts
through from the façade to the
bar of Caffe Bongo

84

Wakaba, West Hampstead, London

Pawson Silvestrin

Caffe Bongo in the Shibuya district of Tokyo was the first example of Nigel Coates's NATO architecture (Narrative Architecture Today) to leave the drawing board in 1987. Since then **Branson Coates Architecture** have become the darlings of avant-garde Japanese club owners, restaurateurs and retailers. British clients followed, after Coates's extravagant approach to architecture proved to be commercially sound. The spirit of Branson Coates Architecture's humorous approach is well caught in this fashionable Tokyo bar. Set in the ground floor of the Parco department store (the Tokyo equivalent of Selfridges), Caffe Bongo is entered under a battered Boeing-707-like wing complete with jet engines jutting into the street. The stage-set interior is an extravaganza of architectural curios, ancient Rome colliding with the Post-Holocaust school of design. Branson Coates Architecture shipped out a team of fellow craft workers to achieve the high level of craft that an older generation of architects believes does not belong with this seemingly anarchic approach to design. The truth is that Nigel Coates, no matter how fashionable, has more in common with the English Arts and Crafts tradition or the Festival of Britain spirit than he does with a later British architecture that eschewed detail for bombastic effect.

Opposite **Bar: airline seats under mock jet engines in Caffe Bongo**

Above **Private dining-room**

At Wakaba (1987) the architects have broken all the laws of conventional restaurant design. The restaurant is entirely free of clutter. There are no furnishings of any kind to distract from the colourful, sculpted food. Pawson and Silvestrin are completely at odds with the return to colourful materials and decoration that has characterized British architecture of the late 1980s. The plan is simplicity itself. The main dining-room, interrupted by a single pillar, is flanked by a private dining area set behind a screen and a counter at which the sushi chef demonstrates his craft to mesmerized customers.

Above Main dining-room

Opposite Unostentatious
entrance. Façade has a subtly
curved translucent glass screen

Joe's Café, Brompton Cross, London

Jiricna Kerr Associates

When Joe's Café opened in Brompton Cross in 1985, it was virtually empty every lunchtime and every evening. The unfamiliar delicacy of the cooking, lavish bills and unrelenting architecture seemed to keep the wealthy local residents and shoppers at bay. Today there is always a long queue to find a table. Fortunately Eva Jiricna's beautifully detailed black, white and steel interior has proved to be immensely durable. Joe's Café, owned by fashion designer Joseph Ettedgui, was meant to be uncompromising in every way and very glamorous. Eva Jiricna has explored to the full her refined repertoire of High-Tech detailing, here far more expressive than usual.

Above **Bar and entrance lobby**

Opposite **Two-level restaurant**

Ground floor plan

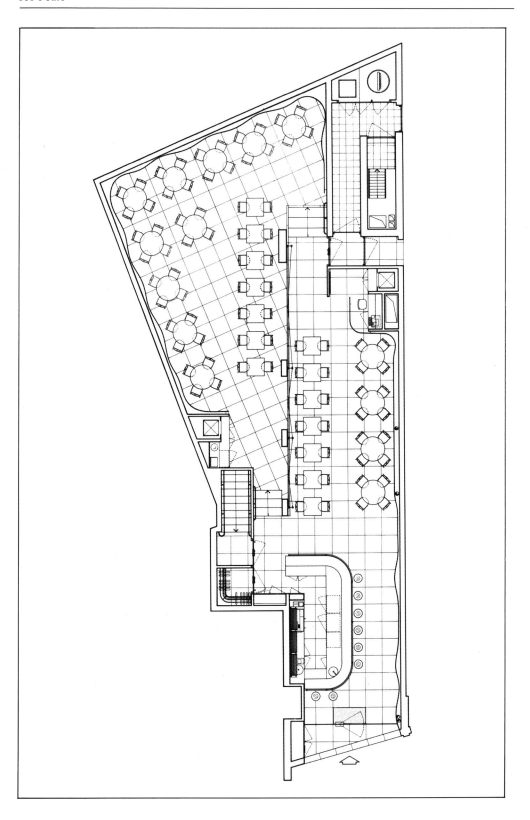

Legends, Mayfair, London

Jiricna Kerr Associates

The new interior of Legends, the Old Burlington Street night club, opened in 1985, replacing an earlier interior for the same club. Legends is an expensive discothèque, a place where people come to talk as well as dance. So Jiricna's interior features several points of rest, most prominently the grand central stairs leading down from the bar to the dance floor which stop off at a large mezzanine level on the way. Here revellers can talk and watch the proceedings without being caught up in the frenzy of the dance floor. Dramatic stairs are one of Eva Jiricna's hallmarks. These provide the pivot around which her immaculately detailed interiors turn. They also encourage a sense of movement and, in this case, an occasion for people to meet, chat and move on without feeling trapped.

For a discothèque the design is remarkably restrained. The drama is found in the structural elements of the interior, such as the cheesegrater steel cladding, rather than in applied decoration. Thus the guests are kept in sharp focus. The fact that the management have no intention of changing Eva Jiricna's interior proves that her design – dramatically modern, exciting and yet crafted and solid – has been recognized as a far more valid approach than ritzy decoration that has to be renewed every few years. Legends, like most of Eva Jiricna's interiors, will remain fashionable because of its timeless drama.

Grand stairs and cheesegrater columns

95

Above Bar

Opposite Bar of Bingo Bango Bongo designed with artist Bruce McLean

Overleaf Corner of Le Champenois bar: mural by Mark Wickham

As with other young British practices, such as Branson Coates Architecture, **David Chipperfield and Partners** have made their reputation through small and highly fashionable projects that have attracted wide publicity. The **Bingo Bango Bongo** nightclub in **Tokyo** (1986) is a simple interior relying as much on broad bands of colour and Bruce McLean's dramatic murals as it does on its low-key architecture. Where young British architects once moved from small housing schemes towards grand projects like museums, today the route, certainly in Japan, a country which has enjoyed a love affair with avant-garde British architecture in the latter half of the 1980s, is through fashion, retail and entertainment.

Corney and Barrow, City of London

Wickham Associates

Corney and Barrow in the City of London (1983) was the first in a series of striking restaurants designed by Julyan Wickham during the 1980s. Restaurants have rarely been so overtly architectural in character. Owned by the long-established firm of City wine merchants of the same name, Corney and Barrow comprises a glittering champagne bar fronting Moorgate, a library-like wine shop cut through a bland 1960s speculative office block and a plush underground restaurant. The stairs leading down to the restaurant are in part an architectural illusion created by an imaginative use of floor-to-ceiling mirrors. Wickham designed many of the fittings and furniture in Corney and Barrow. Bars, light fittings and handrails are all characteristic of Wickham's thorough-going and imaginative approach to detailing. When Corney and Barrow opened, it seemed remarkable that strait-laced bankers should have come to terms so quickly with such a radical new interior. However, the quality of finish and the use of rich traditional materials give this interior an old-fashioned character, proving that a sense of continuity and tradition can be achieved in the design of City institutions without the need to ape established styles. Five years on Corney and Barrow has remained unchanged.

Opposite **Mirror image at Corney and Barrow**

Above **Illusions in basement-level restaurant**

Kensington Place, Notting Hill Gate, London

Wickham Associates

Opened in 1988, Kensington Place is a bustling Anglo-French brasserie catering to young and wealthy Londoners. Despite being housed at the bottom of a dreary office block on a busy junction at Notting Hill Gate, it is always full. Much of the appeal stems from Julyan and Tess Wickham's design, a high ceilinged, cavernous room interrupted only by dramatic white pylons which are clamped round the existing concrete columns and provide subtle ambient light as well as storage for glasses, cups and saucers and cutlery. A very ordinary rectangular space has been transformed into a glamorous brasserie by simple techniques handled deftly. Lighting is indirect, from the pylons and from the curved ceiling baffle hung over the bar – one of Wickham's best. A rich wood block floor, mirrors, a mural by the architect's brother and Wickham's own controversial chairs. The whole interior is in full view of passing traffic, the exterior wall nothing more than pavement-to-ceiling sheets of plate glass. Characteristic of Wickham's ability to transform the least interesting space into a distinctly Modern, yet overtly glamorous experience, Kensington Place exemplifies an approach to architecture that encourages a new generation to reconsider the values of Modernism.

Above 1960s ceiling and columns hidden behind new pylons and curved baffles

Opposite Entrance, bar and pylon detail

Axonometric drawing

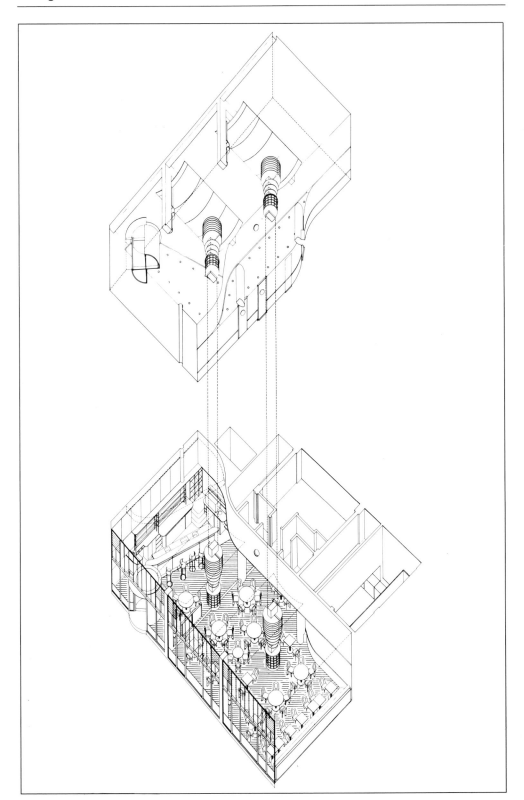

Le Champenois, City of London

Wickham Associates

Julyan Wickham does not want to go down in history as a restaurant designer. However, he has consistently produced some of the most sophisticated restaurants in Britain and, though he is now working on a much broader architectural canvas than before, he is still designing new examples of the genre. Completed in 1985, Le Champenois is the last, to date, in a line of City restaurants which make a virtue of being tucked into tight street frontages and hide their bulk in basements. Le Champenois is an altogether more relaxed design than Wickham's earlier City brasseries, making considerable use of bright paintwork and murals. Typically, Wickham has introduced a complex of curves into the plan, furniture and surfaces that encourages an effortless flow of diners from street to seat. So many restaurants are simply rectangular shops crowded with chairs and tables. Quite often they are enjoyable examples of the decorator's art. Rarely, as with Le Champenois, are they architecture.

Serpentine ceiling and walls; view into main restaurant

Zanzibar, Covent Garden, London

Julyan Wickham

The Zanzibar club opened in 1976 when Covent Garden was London's most fashionable area. Since then Soho has reasserted its primacy. Zanzibar was the first of a new generation of clubs catering to media people tired of smoky pubs, glitzy cocktail bars and the stringent rules of established clubs which, in all likelihood, did not want them as members anyway. Julyan Wickham and Tchaik Chassay's design for Zanzibar set a precedent for this new wave of exclusive London clubs. Wickham's snaking bar, designed so that those perched along its length could watch, wave and call to fellow drinkers, became the architect's stock-in-trade for some of the most memorable restaurant interiors of the 1980s. Zanzibar is a simply planned and decorated interior. Wickham and Chassay lavished their budget on the glittering bar and counter area to create maximum dramatic impact for minimal outlay. A little faded now, this influential bar has become a stopping-off point for ageing public relations and advertising executives.

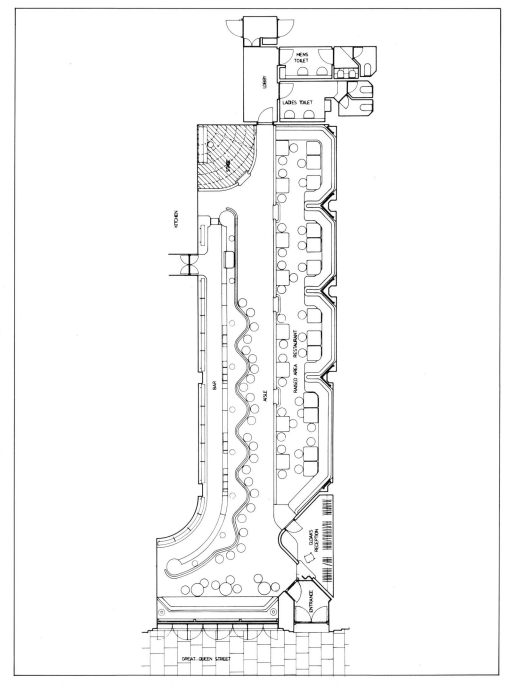

Plan: first example of Wickham's snaking bar

106

Public Buildings

Despite the decline of the public sector, a whole new generation of civic centres, leisure complexes, art galleries, museums and sports halls have been commissioned throughout the 1980s. Leisure, along with retailing and heritage (the packaging of more and more everyday British life into museums and 'interpretation centres' for the benefit of tourists), has become one of the key concerns of a society faced with mass unemployment. Rather like Imperial Rome's policy of 'bread and circuses', local authorities have tried to keep people occupied and out of mischief. Architectural practices like the Newcastle-based Faulkner-Brown, Watkinson, Hendy and Stonor have created extravagant programmes for High-Tech swimming pools alongside such handsome public works as the new civic centre at Chester-le-Street in County Durham (1983; pp. 66-67).

Nicholas Grimshaw and Partners were responsible for the dramatic new ice rink in Oxford (1985; pp. 110-11) which opened during a new-found popular craze for ice skating brought about by the international sporting successes of the British champions Torvill and Dean. The building was significant in the story of a newly sports- and health-conscious society in that its design allowed passers-by a full view into the glittering ice palace, encouraging casual observers to enter.

Local authority architecture of any distinction has been sparse throughout the 1980s, save in the case of the remarkable Winchester office of the Hampshire County Architect's Department. The County Architect, Colin Stansfield-Smith has maintained an approach to architecture throughout the decade that has attracted international interest and produced some of the most humane public buildings in Europe. The John Darling Mall in Eastleigh (1986) and the primary school at Tadley (1984-87; p. 19) demonstrate how public authority projects can still occupy a central position in architectural design. The John Darling Mall marks a significant departure

from the usual prison- or hospital-like institutional building provided for the disabled.

The university building programme, which had provided so much work for the best British architects in the 1960s and 1970s, has been greatly reduced in the 1980s. Nevertheless, at least two distinguished buildings have resulted. The first was the new hall of residence at Worcester College, Oxford, by MacCormac Jamieson Pritchard and Wright (pp. 120-23) and the second Rick Mather's University of East Anglia computer science building in Norwich (1981-85; pp. 124-26).

By contrast, the vast increase in new museums is an international phenomenon that has kept architects busy throughout the 1980s. Those cities which had historically displayed their wealth and culture in the construction of churches and palaces now vie with each other to build the greatest number of museums. Frankfurt in West Germany has led the way during the decade by employing architects of international standing: Hans Hollein, Richard Meier and O. M. Ungers among them. In Stuttgart, Stirling and Wilford produced their 1980s masterpiece, the Staatsgalerie (p. 32), the design for which raised this museum from a humble place in the popularity league of German museums to prime position within a few months of its opening.

In Britain, one of the best received and yet most lonely buildings is the Burrell Collection by Barry Gasson Architects (1971-83; pp. 115-19). Barry Gasson (b. 1935) won the commission in competition in 1971 and spent several long years working more or less by himself on its design. Highly individual and crafted, the Burrell Collection, set some miles out of Glasgow city centre, is easily one of Britain's most popular new museums and the winner of many awards.

Museum culture seems to have taken a real grip on the official imagination. Throughout the country existing museums have been extended, renovated and redeveloped. Arup Associates were asked to remodel the Imperial War Museum, Lambeth (formerly Bethlehem Royal Hospital or 'Bedlam') in 1986; Stirling and Wilford added the colourful and abstract Clore Gallery (1980-86), housing the Turner bequest, to the Edwardian, Baroque Tate on the Thames Embankment and have refurbished a part of the Piranesian Albert Dock buildings in Liverpool for the Tate of the North (1988).

The most controversial plans for a new museum arose from the long-delayed extension to the National Gallery on the north side of London's Trafalgar Square. A bomb-site to the west of William Wilkins's Neo-Greek gallery (1832-38) provided a natural space for a much-needed new wing, but progress on new work was considerably delayed. A competition held in 1984 for the design of an extension generated one of the most bitter architectural disputes in many years.

The dismissal by the Prince of Wales of the original Post-Modern design by Ahrends, Burton and Koralek led, after a second competition, to the appointment of the American Post-Modern guru, Robert Venturi. Venturi's design was a soft-focused play on the original Wilkins's building, but it fell between two stools, being neither convincingly Classical, nor inventively Post-Modern. Perhaps the saving grace was the design of the traditional rooms for displaying Italian Renaissance paintings.

In the 1980s traditional features – smaller rooms and decoration – have begun to be reintroduced into art-gallery interiors. Only a decade earlier, architects and museum curators had favoured large, featureless, open-plan galleries, symbols of the growing emptiness of public architecture. Though suitable for displaying large-scale works of contemporary art, these galleries did not present other collections at their best and were, on the whole, unpopular with the public. By contrast, Stirling's treatment of interiors at the Clore Gallery, the Stuttgart Staatsgalerie and at Liverpool in the 1980s has been highly successful, when judged by the number of visitors to these museums.

Ice rink, Oxford

Nicholas Grimshaw and Partners

This exuberant building owes its dramatic profile to the nature of the land on which it perches. Patrons here truly skate on thin ice because the Oxford ice rink rests on marshland. A heavyweight building of brick and concrete, if not prohibited, would have been difficult to engineer, and so Nicholas Grimshaw and Partners came up with the idea of a lightweight steel and glass building, the weight of which is spread lightly across the site. It stands rather like some High-Tech schooner anchored to a bank. As such the ice rink (1985) with its lofty masts and taut steel rigging is unmistakable, advertising itself from a great distance. It is also the only notable building along a particularly dismal stretch of the Oxford one-way traffic system. One of the most enjoyable aspects of this Meccano-like building is the way it allows passers-by to glance through the huge windows overlooking the road. Grimshaw specializes in designing buildings that look like gigantic toys. His design for Homebase DIY store on the Great West Road in Brentford, for example, resembles a grounded glider.

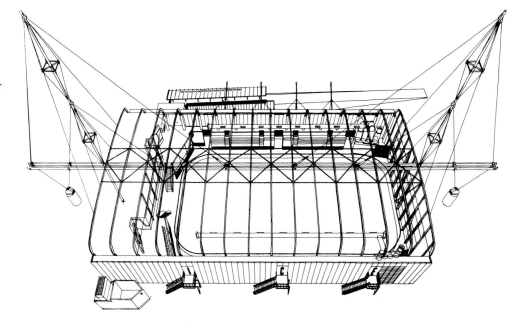

Top Roof held up by dominant masts

Right Cut-away view through ice rink

Opposite Schooner come to berth: ice rink from behind

Whitechapel Art Gallery, London

Colquhoun Miller and Partners

The Whitechapel Art Gallery completed in 1901, represents one of the highpoints of the British flirtation with Art Nouveau. Yet behind its elaborate facade, it was never anything more than an architecturally void two-storey warehouse. In 1985 Colquhoun and Miller were commissioned to extend and bring fresh life into the gallery. The architects have managed to add a functional, yet far from characterless, extension at the back which comprises accommodation for administration, education and catering. Best of all, the revamped building benefits from a highly articulate and well-finished elevation. The Townsend galleries have been changed subtly, yet to dramatic effect. New wooden floors, discreet downlighting, movable ceiling-hung screens and several coats of brilliant white paint have created the desired impression. A new staircase lit on the first floor by a distinctive oriel window leads up to the mezzanine cafeteria. The building was always bathed in a wash of daylight, from above and from the sides; the architects have added light-sensitive blinds but otherwise left the gallery in a state that its original designer would have been proud of. Colquhoun and Miller represent a rational and pragmatic current in the choppy waters of British architecture and this handsome gallery renovation shows how unpretentious architecture can often be the most satisfying.

Above Top-floor gallery lit from above

Opposite New stairwell oriel and bow window to restaurant

Right Main gallery looking towards entrance

Below left Townsend's restored Art Nouveau façade

Below right First-floor restaurant

Burrell Collection, Glasgow

Barry Gasson Architects

A quick glance at the plan of the Burrell Collection – a giant cheese dish abstract – could convince anyone who has not visited this remarkable building that it must be some quintessentially 1960s concrete dinosaur. The reality could hardly be more different. The Burrell Collection is a reticent building that weaves a delightful tapestry with the threads of architecture and nature. The museum is built from largely natural materials – red sandstone and timber – and sits on a sloping site in a mature woodland. The interior planting and trunk-like columns supporting the exposed timber trusses of the great glazed roofs add to the notion, not so fanciful, that a visit to this museum is like a walk in the woods, or, given its rich contents, an educational stroll through some Arcadian grove. A cross between a great, medieval monastery and a nineteenth-century conservatory or winter garden, the Burrell Collection is a distinctive yet understated building. It took twelve years to complete, starting with a competition held for its design in 1971. The winning team comprised three young Cambridge architects: Barry Gasson, John Meunier and Brett Andreson. Despite the museum's immense solidity, the lasting impression is of Sir William Burrell's collection of precious objects, spanning 4,000 years, set wherever possible against a changing natural backdrop of chestnuts and sycamores, bluebells and bracken.

Restaurant seen from park

Above Displays as close to
nature as possible

Opposite Cross axis through
Burrell Collection, emphasizing
daylight

Overleaf Galleries designed as a
continuation of a walk in the
woods

Sainsbury Building, Worcester College, Oxford

MacCormac, Jamieson, Pritchard and Wright

Opposite **Main entrance from lakeside**

Left **Modernism with a traditional face: Arts-and-Crafts-like timber fittings**

Right **Stepped contours seen from lakeside walkway**

The low-lying, many-roofed Sainsbury Building (1983) in the beautiful grounds of Worcester College is one of the most successful in an approach to architectural design that *The Architectural Review* has labelled 'Romantic Pragmatism'. The term is applied to buildings that adopt a vernacular vocabulary without abandoning the basic tenet of Modern Movement architecture – that a building's plan should be strictly functional and its elevations should rise up from the dictates of the plan and not from those of fashion. The net result is almost medieval or Gothic in conception. The building's plan develops from complex clusters of L-shaped rooms gathered around roof terraces and gardens outside, kitchens and dining-rooms inside. The clusters form the basic building block. This approach is a fresh interpretation of the traditional staircase or corridor layout adopted by Oxbridge colleges. The rooms and roofs appear to grow organically out of a fortified wall overlooking a moat (the lake) which give the Sainsbury Building a sense of medieval security and Arts and Crafts design, a feeling reinforced by the well-crafted interiors. Rather than specify furniture from a catalogue, the architects have designed their own, part of their complete approach to planning the building.

SECTION A A

SECTION BB

SECTIONS

**Sections through Sainsbury
Building**

Organic nature of building: it will age naturally and gracefully

Computer science building, University of East Anglia, Norwich

Rick Mather Architects

Courtyard

Rick Mather's brand of icy cool Modernism was reserved for a small number of house conversions, shops and sophisticated Chinese restaurants until he was commissioned by the University of East Anglia to design these buildings, completed in 1985, for the Schools of Education Information Systems and Climatic Research Unit. Mather's first large-scale project has been described as a 'Neo-Classic *palazzo*'. The reality reveals smoothly clad, regular Modern buildings arranged in a severe group around a courtyard. The new schools fit into a striking body of radical buildings that include Denys Lasdun's Inca pyramid halls of residence dating from the 1960s and Norman Foster's High-Tech Classical Sainsbury Centre for the Visual Arts (1978). Mather has chosen to break the geometry of his façades in response to functional demands, so that although windows and bay widths are essentially regular, larger windows or projecting bays are used when the rooms call for them. Behind the smooth pale-grey and blue tiled elevations, Mather has created an interior that surprises with its rich sequence of spaces and its use of natural light wherever possible. These new university buildings might look severe, but, as befits a centre for computer studies, they are 'user friendly'.

AXONOMETRIC LOOKING WEST

Axonometric Drawing

Circular tower is pivot to new
buildings

Henley Regatta headquarters, Henley

Terry Farrell Partnership

Terry Farrell began his career as a practitioner of High-Tech design with Nicholas Grimshaw. Since going his separate way with the Terry Farrell Partnership, he has enthusiastically endorsed the architecture of American Post-Modernism, most notably that of the influential Princeton architect Michael Graves. Farrell has also gone on record saying that one of the greatest influences on his architecture is Walt Disney. Most of Farrell's work is in central London. However, this delightful riverside Classical temple in Henley, dating from 1985, is Post-Modernism on another plane. Neither too colourful nor too brash, the headquarters of the Henley Regatta is the most delightful building Farrell has yet produced. Growing from a handsome and richly articulated brick base, the headquarters takes the form of a Greek temple. Despite the American colour scheme, the building appears muscular and full of charm, an elegant addition to a famous and much-used stretch of the Thames.

Top River frontage

Above left Close-up of Post-Modern Classical façade; boats moor underneath

Above right Riverfront at night

Howard Building, Downing College, Cambridge

Erith and Terry

Over eighty per cent of the cost of the new Howard Building (1988) at Downing College has been lavished on its Portland and Ketton stone walls. In that sense alone this simple building – basically a lecture theatre at first-floor level open to the timber roof – is old-fashioned. This was precisely what the dons of Downing College wanted, a building that would form a happy marriage with the existing Neo-Classical pavilions by William Wilkins and E. M. Barry. Typical of Quinlan Terry's style, the well-crafted façades are highly mannered and rather fussy when compared with Wilkins's chaste Grecian style thus giving the Howard Building the look of a very expensive doll's house. Perhaps more satisfying than the elaborate north front is the much plainer south elevation characterized by the giant Corinthian pilasters that frame either side of the façade and the baseless Roman Doric colonnade. Nevertheless, the disjunction between the two principal façades is a curious one. More unsettling is the fact that the Doric columns echoed inside the ground floor are lower than those supporting the colonnade, so missing the opportunity of creating a grove of columns marching through the depth of the building. For all its oddities, Sir John Summerson calls the Howard Building 'a useful job that radiates charm and remarkable talent. As a subject for debate it will afford endless entertainment. And why not?'

Above Terry's feminine building (right) in contrast with Wilkins's masculine Neo-Classicism

Left Garden front could belong to a different building

Opposite Highly mannered and well-wrought end façade

Shops

The boom in retailing in the 1980s, confirmation of Napoleon's dictum that the British are a nation of shopkeepers, has occurred at the same time as the rise of what journalists like to call 'designer culture'. In the 1980s whatever is new and colourful is prefixed by the term 'designer'; the British travel by 'designer train' to buy 'designer clothes' in 'designer shops'. Although this nomenclature is banal in the extreme, the rise of designer culture has led to a considerable amount of work for young architects setting up in practice, nearly all of which is concentrated in London, the British centre of the fashion and design buisness.

As a result the 1980s have witnessed dozens of intriguing experiments in shop design. Inevitably most of these buildings are ephemeral, vanishing as businesses go bankrupt, expand into new premises or alter their image. The changes in style have been sudden. The High-Tech or Post-Modern look of the early 1980s has given way to raw experiments in 'Creative Salvage' – the best-known example being Ron Arad's One Off shops in Covent Garden – and later to all things Japanese. Perhaps the Japanese style is most satisfying to architects concerned with the play of light on simple shapes, with natural materials, simplicity, and craftsmanship, who look back wistfully to the early days of Modernism. It is impossible to escape the *Existenzminimum* or Japanese-influenced shop in city centres at the end of the 1980s. Some of the best examples include shops for the Japanese fashion designer Issey Miyake in Sloane Street, London (1985) by David Chipperfield and Ken Armstrong; for the same client in London's Old Brompton Road (1987; pp. 140-41) by Stanton and Williams; for Michiko Koshino in Wells Street, London (1984-85; pp. 136-37) by Pierre d'Avoine; and for Yohji Yamamoto (1987), also in Sloane Street, by Munkenbeck and Marshall.

Fashion and architecture now form a natural alliance, even though they were considered mutually exclusive twenty years ago. Several of the famous fashion design have been trained as architects, including Britain's Rifat Ozbek, Italy's Gianfranco Ferre and America's Zoran. But British architects have been designing clothes fo many years, long before the 'designer' fashion boom of the 1980s. The Arts and Crafts architect C. F. A. Voysey (1857–1944), for instance, fashioned his own cuffless suits. Lapels and turn-ups served only to gather dust and so, in the tidy and highly individualist Voysey creed, had to banned.

High-Tech interiors have not stayed i fashion for long. As with buildings in the same genre, they require skilled craftmanship to look convincing. Put together crudely by interior design practi seizing on the look, they seem merely 'glitzy'. The most successful designs in th vein are the work of Eva Jiricna (b. 1938) who is responsible for the widely copied fashion shops for Joseph Ettedgui (1985; pp. 138-39) as well as for his restaurant Joe's Café (1985; pp. 92-94). When the well-known Harrods department store decided to sell young fashion lines in 198 Jiricna Kerr (with Jan Kaplicky) were asked to create a High-Tech floor.

Foster Associates produced two elemental shops for the fashion designer Katharine Hamnett, one a conventional shop, the other a stark warehouse reache by a dramatic steel bridge from an unprepossessing entrance. The most impressive example of this style, Sainsbu supermarket in Camden Town by Nicho Grimshaw and Partners opened to a mixe reception in 1989.

If design and fashion shops have beer compressed mostly into the cosmopolita confines of central London, the whole of Britain has been witness to the spread of hypermarkets and shopping malls. Pract such as the Building Design Partnership, Bernard Engle Partnership, and Chapma Taylor Partners have been extremely bus producing both city-centre and out-of-to shopping complexes. Perhaps the most dramatic and influential of the new wave of shopping malls is the Building Design Partnership's Ealing Centre (1985; pp. 144-46) in west London. A vast area of shops, supermarkets, car parking space, sports and other social facilities are clustered together in the guise of some fantastic, medieval walled town, complete with towers, gables, decorative wrought ironwork and crafted brickwork. The Ealing Centre is by far the biggest building in this handsome suburb, dominating even the lofty parish church and Gothic Revival town hall. The shopping mall of the 1980s is quite clearly the cathedral of the late twentieth century, usurping the role of the nineteenth-century railway station and the eighteenth-century assembly rooms.

The consumer boom has seen a vast increase in expenditure on DIY (do it yourself), which has necessitated the construction of hundreds of simply decorated warehouses on the edge of every major town. By the late 1980s it appeared unlikely that any architect would be approached to rethink these banal designs. Even so, a commission has gone to Nicholas Grimshaw and Partners to produce a new Homebase warehouse in north London. Aside from the functional finesse of the Grimshaw building, the client is well aware of the advertising potential of such a dramatic building. Although constructed in a very different style, the Grimshaw warehouse is reminiscent in spirit of the flamboyant Art Deco factories of the early 1930s – such as the Hoover Building by Wallis Gilbert and Partners – that line the Great West Road and the Western Avenue in west London.

Michiko Koshino shop, Soho, London

Pierre d'Avoine Architects

This shop for the Japanese fashion designer Michiko Koshino dating from 1984 is tucked away in the rag trade district behind Oxford Street. It was the first successful Japanese-influenced shop interior in London. Designed by Pierre d'Avoine (with Jonathan Stickland and William White), the Michiko shop is a well-crafted shelter for a range of dramatic and inventive clothes. An angled limed oak bridge from the entrance leads across a moat of black slate into a white interior bathed in soft light from concealed sources. Clothes hang from swivelling black steel gibbets on one side of the shop, while on the other side smaller items rest on prominent white shelves supported by columns and beams. The rather ethereal atmosphere of this small but significant shop is heightened by inventive details such as the ceiling which appears to float, changing rooms separated by screens of milky glass and a section of wall that pivots to give access to the storeroom below. Subtle and in good taste, like the clothes it cradles, the Michiko shop has led d'Avoine to design a chain of menswear shops for Michiko in Tokyo.

Opposite Abstract simplicity of shop contrasts with florid Edwardian façade

Above Clothes dramatically displayed

137

Joseph shop, Knightsbridge, London

Jiricna Kerr Associates

Joseph pour la Maison opened on Sloane Street in 1985. The black-and-white and chromed steel of the basement café in this shrine to matt black household accessories (the height of fashion at the time) was a clever accompaniment to the goods on sale above. When first opened, the café, designed by Eva Jiricna, attracted a crowd of wealthy young fashion victims who sat brooding and silent while studying the cut of each other's clothes over an untouched *cappuccino*. Since then the atmosphere has become more jolly, as Joseph has returned to colour and his style has become popular with the well-heeled and high-heeled as well as the intensely fashion-conscious. Jiricna's Classical interior relies on simple black-and-white surfaces highlighted on the shop floor by walls of translucent profiled glass and in the café by a backdrop of mirrors, against which undisturbed ranks of Perrier and Coca-Cola bottles act as modern sculpture. The plan of the Joseph shop is perfectly simple, while Jiricna's detailing is, as ever, sophisticated and well executed. If every object in the shop looks worth the sometimes alarming price tags, it is largely the doing of Eva Jiricna.

Opposite Dramatic simplicity of interior heightens clothes on display

Above Highly wrought banister detail

Issey Miyake shop, Knightsbridge, London

Stanton and Williams

Issey Miyake, the Japanese fashion guru, designs abstract sculptural clothes that need precious little in the way of architectural support. Stanton and Williams's Issey Miyake shop in London's Old Brompton Road (1987) has a well-crafted Minimal interior that serves Miyake's clothes well. Stanton and Williams have proved their expertise in designing imaginatively detailed, small-scale projects that have raised what have mostly been temporary structures into the realm of architecture. The heraldic tents that stood outside the Tate Gallery in 1983 and the Gothic exhibition held at the Royal Academy in 1987 are two memorable examples. The quietly dramatic Miyake shop, which could just as well be in Tokyo, is essentially a more permanent exhibition for the Japanese designer.

Above Architecture subservient to goods on display

Opposite Simplicity, texture and light: the essence of Japanese style

Katharine Hamnett shop, Knightsbridge, London

Branson Coates Architecture

The importance of designing a shop on Sloane Street, one of the most exclusive row of fashion shops anywhere in the world, is obvious. A shop-front here is an advertisement for architectural style and skill. Katharine Hamnett's last shop was designed by Foster Associates whose elegant, sparse, High-Tech approach could hardly have been more different from the crafted flamboyance of Branson Coates Architecture. The whimsical, yet ordered, design of this new shop, completed late in 1988, is a rich foil to Hamnett's severe, if sexy, couture. The shop-front draws more attention than most perhaps, largely through its elaborate and fashionable display of tropical fish. The aquariums were embellished by radical architects' favourite craftsman Tom Dixon who works almost exclusively in welded steel. Although seemingly carefree, the architects' decoration is distinguished from all-too-common pale imitations by its undeniable quality. Nigel Coates has assembled a team of contemporary designers and craftsmen and women who work closely with his practice to ensure that even the most bizarre idea is translated into something solid, workable and enduring.

Stage-set shop-front; aquariums for tropical fish designed by Tom Dixon

**Interior dialogue between
Coates's flamboyant architecture
and Hamnett's severe couture**

Ealing Centre, Ealing Broadway, London

Building Design Partnership

The shopping mall has become one of the dominant building types of the 1980s. The Ealing Centre, designed by Britain's largest architectural practice, Building Design Partnership (BDP), and completed in 1985, was one of the first of the colossal buildings to be designed with an architectural theme in mind instead of being just a brutally functional response to the need to provide the maximum amount of undercover retail space. BDP chose a bizarre fairy-tale Gothic style, picking up on the Neo-Gothic grandeur of the nearby Ealing Town Hall. The towers of the car park rise high above the existing shops and houses, demonstrating the importance of shopping as Britain's favourite civic and cultural activity in the 1980s. The Ealing Centre plays with architectural styles in a humourless way. The sports hall is designed to look medieval, the offices a curious free-style Edwardian. The architects commissioned craft-made ironwork and other rustic details, yet these only add to the theme-park character of the Ealing Centre. However, buildings like this have proved to be immensely popular, a fact that can only encourage architects in the 1990s to play outrageous games in the centre of our cities. Brute concrete might have given way to colourful bricks and bright colours, but the sheer bulk of modern shopping malls makes them architectural predators.

Above **Looking towards sports complex (centre)**

Opposite **Pseudo-traditional office façades**

**Main square dominated by twin
lift and stair towers servicing car
park**

Industrial Buildings

In a way it is ironic that while many of the most dazzling new British buildings of the 1980s – the Lloyd's headquarters by Richard Rogers and Partners (p. 22), the Hongkong and Shanghai Bank by Foster Associates – have owed much to industrial imagery and technology, the most satisfying new industrial buildings are built from traditional materials. The reasoning, however, is not difficult to follow.

Attempts to design factories and warehouses from the late 1970s in a style that borrowed from industrial imagery led to immediate problems. Glistening new High-Tech sheds, made from sophisticated sandwich construction panels, whether of plastic or aluminium, are prone to damage from lorries and fork-lift trucks, among other industrial hazards, and from deterioration caused by Britain's wet climate. Water or condensation seeping into sophisticated cladding systems can, and has, destroyed them very easily. A High-Tech warehouse, seemingly appropriate for its job, is destined for a relatively short life. Yet with money and craftsmanship such buildings can be both exciting to look at and tough enough to withstand the rigours of a workaday life. It was the realization by clients and architects that High-Tech buildings could not be low-cost solutions for industry that led to a move back to traditional construction, or at least to traditional cladding. Nevertheless, at their best High-Tech buildings have caught the excitement of the industrial process.

It is ironic that the components usually reflect the world of pre-war engineering: split pins and tie-rods, drilled steel struts and crossbars. A building designed in this way would house a company manufacturing something as modern as silicon chips (for example Richard Rogers and Partners' elegant Inmos factory in Gwent, South Wales, 1982). When applied to a car distribution centre such as the Renault warehouse, Swindon (Foster Associates, 1983), the architecture has obvious echoes in the product it shelters.

While undeniably glamorous, such buildings demand a real commitment by the owners who are effectively charged with repainting them on a regular basis to keep them in pristine condition. Two of the most elegant are Michael Hopkins's Greene King brewery at Bury St Edmunds (1979) and the same architect's Schlumberger Research Laboratories outside Cambridge (1985; pp. 152-155 and 157). Another is Nicholas Grimshaw and Partners' printing works for the Financial Times in the former East India Docks on the Isle of Dogs (completed 1988; pp. 158-59).

Perhaps the biggest irony of these intriguing, richly detailed, and highly crafted buildings lies in the fact that their design is a homage to the great Victorian engineers and manufacturers who made Britain the workshop of the world. By the 1980s Britain has become a service economy relying heavily on international trade, banking, insurance, North Sea oil, retailing and tourism to create wealth. It is no longer a manufacturing nation.

Brick warehouses have proved tougher than those clad optimistically in plastic or aluminium. The case of Aztec West (pp. 150-51) demonstrates vividly how buildings clad in traditional materials are easier to assemble on site (prefabricated components do not necessarily fit together as they should do), more resilient to rough treatment and more graceful as they age. John Outram, in particular, has shown in the simple warehouses at Kensal Road, London (1982), and at Aztec West, Bristol (1987) how industrial buildings can add to the urban landscape rather than detract from it.

Most architects have resorted to playing with the past in the design of industrial buildings in the 1980s. Visual clichés include the use of flowing, primary-coloured, plastic cladding, colourful doors and large areas of glass. It is rare to find industrial buildings that match the sophistication and noble grandeur of either the First World War airship sheds at Cardington, Bedfordshire or the 1940s

Semtex rubber factory in Brynmawr by the Architects' Co-Partnership. Among the most distinguished in this vein are the Shotts steel factory (1982) by Ahrends, Burton and Koralek and the Dana Woods factory by Shalev and Evans in Bromley, Kent (1983).

An encouraging development in the decade has been the gradual reappearance of the factory as a showpiece of a manufacturer's corporate philosophy and products. In the extreme case of Linn Products, the Glasgow-based manufacturers of high-quality record decks and audio equipment, a new factory in Eaglesham, nine miles south of Glasgow,

was budgeted to cost more than the company's annual turnover at the time of commissioning in 1984. The result is a functional, yet glamorous, building designed by Richard Rogers and Partners and completed by the Clydeside practice Mackenzie and Partners.

In contrast, buildings such as nuclear power stations in the 1980s have been made to look brutal and terrifying in a manner fit for the hostile process they house and the threat of universal destruction they pose. Perhaps it is right that no attempt has been made to embellish a building type that is at best considered a necessary evil.

Aztec West, Bristol, Avon

Campbell Zogolovitch Wilkinson and Gough

CZWG specialize in flamboyant buildings that could be described as 1980s Art Deco. Sometimes vulgar, often witty, the practice likes to deck out plain building types in colourful clothes. Piers Gough belies his critics by describing the practice's work as 'B-movie architecture'. One of the architects' most restrained buildings, completed in 1987, is also one of their best: a speculatively built suite of industrial offices dressed in overtly Art Deco garb in the grounds of Aztec West, Bristol's High-Tech business park. Echoing Art Deco factories as well as the dramatic, prefabricated, Classical housing of Ricardo Bofill's Taller de Arquitectura, these twin blocks exhibit a true sense of the theatrical and represent a considerable change of heart on the part of developers of Aztec West. Earlier buildings on the site were either 'Slick-Tech' sheds or banal design-build boxes. The two identical CZWG buildings face each other across a circular courtyard designed to make it easy for cars and vans to turn around.

Opposite Cinematic entrance

Above Curved façade thins out to a sharp edge

Schlumberger Research Laboratories, Cambridge

Michael Hopkins and Partners

What prompted Michael Hopkins to produce a building as exuberant as this in flat Cambridgeshire? Certainly there is no obvious functional justification for such a complex of tented roofs and guy ropes. Perhaps it was the flat landscape itself that encouraged the architect to do what his medieval forebears had done at Ely: to build an unmistakable symbol of the times on a site where it can be seen for miles. As the Schlumberger building (1985) is situated in the middle of the countryside, the architect has not had to consider its relationship to neighbouring buildings. Instead he has strung up a building like a giant tent covering a sequence of laboratories and offices. Presumably the structure is either destined for a limited life or the fabric covering the roofs will simply be replaced as and when necessary. Truly flamboyant and quite Gothic in spirit, the Schlumberger building makes a number of romantic connections in the British mind: it is at one and the same time the tent of the desert explorer, the cathedral seen from across the fens, a reminder of the aeroplane struts of American and British bombers that flew in daylight raids from these fields during the mid-1940s. Above all the building conveys a sense of adventure and discovery, while still fulfilling the function for which it was constructed.

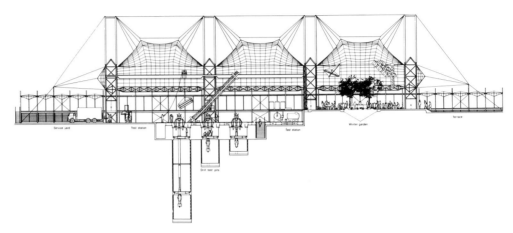

Top Section through research laboratories

Above Like an old plane ready fo take-off: Schlumberger at night

Opposite Fabric roofs stretched by wires held by steel pylons

Overleaf Schlumberger tents at night

152

fantasy provides a welcome and much-loved feature of the town centre. In a similar vein, London is a big enough city to be able to cope with Richard Rogers's dramatic Lloyd's headquarters, just as Paris is with the Pompidou Centre (Piano + Rogers, 1971-77) and with the Eiffel Tower.

However, this element of caution has been important in attempts to civilize the vast urban development schemes that have followed in the wake of Britain's financial and retail boom of the mid-1980s. Architects have been required to squeeze huge under-cover shopping centres into the grain of old towns. Faced with this almost impossible task, they have responded by decorating gargantuan buildings with homely brickwork and crafted details.

But the major opportunities have come with the giant urban sites that have become available for development, primarily in London. The Spitalfields Market site on the edge of the City of London saw a fierce competition between two developers who both turned to imaginative and unusual (in developers' terms) talents. At Spitalfields, in 1985, the Classicists Leon Krier (p. 175) and Quinlan Terry were both invited to demonstrate their ideas of a dense urban centre for the 1990s. Terry had already been commissioned to remodel the riverside centre of Richmond, Surrey, in 1983 in a pot-pourri of eighteenth-century styles (pp. 168 and 170). The rival developer teamed up the big commercial practice of Fitzroy Robinson and Partners with Richard MacCormac. MacCormac's winning scheme was an attempt to tame developers' architecture that elsewhere in London (at Broadgate, at London Bridge City, at King's Cross and at Canary Wharf) is developing into a hearty American game, perfect for Pittsburgh, but out of place in London (pp. 178-79).

However, the danger of inviting distinguished architects to produce major city projects in tandem with developers has been revealed in 1988 with the unveiling of designs for the redevelopment of Paternoster Square (p. 171), which surrounds St Paul's Cathedral. The bombastic designs revealed to the public are far more terrifying than the dull 1950s buildings they are meant to replace. It is small wonder that John Simpson's whimsical Classical revival alternative has won the support of the Prince of Wales. At the end of the 1980s architects still have much to learn about how to work in existing city centres.

Opposite **Office courtyard of Richmond riverside redevelopment. Suspended ceilings and air conditioning behind the façades**

Richmond riverside redevelopment, Surrey

Erith and Terry

Quinlan Terry's redevelopment of Richmond riverside, completed in 1988, is the strongest evidence to date of a Classical revival. Critics agreed that in terms of town planning Terry's contribution to this Thameside town was important, but were divided over the nature of the buildings themselves. What you see looking across from the south bank of the river is a mixture of brand new, restored and remodelled Georgian houses, civic and commercial buildings. However, the highly mannered façades of Terry's new buildings conceal, for the most part, conventional office interiors. Terry has not carried his Classicism through to his interiors which are fitted with suspended ceilings that drop below the window line, air conditioning and strip fluorescent lighting. However, there is no doubt that Terry's scheme has saved Richmond from a number of crass concrete or industrial brick developments that have been planned at various times since the 1960s. There is equally no doubt that the new riverside courtyards, streets and embankment are highly popular public places. Terry has typically indulged in a number of architectural games, borrowing details from his own sketchbooks of Rome and giving fresh twists to Georgian architecture.

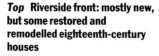

Top Riverside front: mostly new, but some restored and remodelled eighteenth-century houses

Above left Appropriate backdrop to sober monument

Above right West elevation to riverside scheme

170

Paternoster Square redevelopment, City of London

New office technology and a desire to improve the face of the area led to a competition to redevelop Lord Holford's Paternoster Square in 1986. The winning architects, **Arup Associates**, produced a scheme that proved somewhat unintelligible to the general public who seemed to prefer an alternative proposal designed in a mannered Neo-Classical style by **John Simpson and Partners**. Arup Associates withdrew quietly for a year before returning with a clearly understandable scheme that mixed Modernism with Classicism and co-opted Michael Hopkins and Richard MacCormac as joint designers. Simpson's role seems to have been one of reconciling public opinion with Modern architecture in fancy, if not historic, dress. Arup Associates argues that, unlike the Simpson scheme which calls for the return of the close-knit pre-war street pattern around St Paul's, their proposals are in line with those of Wren and Hawksmoor. 'St Paul's is an English Baroque masterpiece, and Wren planned a Baroque and formal precinct for it, not a medieval one.' Nevertheless, St Paul's, its surroundings and the new proposals from Arup Associates have all been appropriate examples of a thoroughly English, if not British, compromise.

Top right Arup Associates' proposed new piazza building facing the west front of St Paul's Cathedral

Right **John Simpson's proposal for Paternoster Square. Painting by Carl Aubin**

Alban Gate, London Wall, London

Terry Farrell Partnership

By 1988 Terry Farrell was rebuilding a considerable part of central London. Currently two major schemes are nearing completion: Alban Gate, a giant, twin-towered, Post-Modern office straddling London Wall and a giant-arched office scheme over the train shed of Charing Cross station. Alban Gate replaces one of the slab-like and smooth-skinned steel-and-glass office towers dating from the late 1950s that parade along London Wall. London Wall, a new road planned in the mid-1950s under the architectural direction of Leslie Martin and Hubert Bennett, was, until the intrusion of Farrell's colossal exercise in extravagant American Post-Modernism, one of the most interesting examples of post-war 'comprehensive redevelopment'. Nikolaus Pevsner found walking through this Corbusian idyll a 'pleasure'. A later generation disagrees. The European urban dream of the 1920s as represented at London Wall in the 1950s is now giving way to a ritzy Art Deco vision imported from the United States.

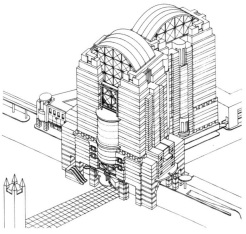

Above Model of Alban Gate. London Wall passes through archway

Left Giant Post-Modern offices straddling London Wall

172

Charing Cross redevelopment, London

Terry Farrell Partnership

The Charing Cross station scheme is subtler than the Alban Gate one. The nine-storey office block now being raised over Charing Cross station creates two dramatic new arches overlooking the Thames. These pick up the tradition of the great Victorian trainsheds. Providing new shops and restaurants along the sides of its colourful and dramatically sculpted bulk, Farrell's Charing Cross development is designed to raise the standards of this fascinating, yet undeniably sordid, part of central London.

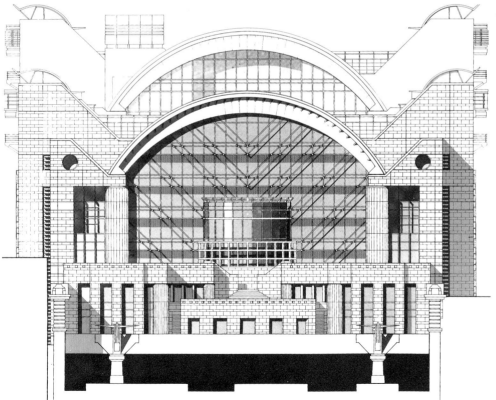

Top **Model of Charing Cross development viewed from the riverside**

Right **South or river frontage of Farrell's remodelled Charing Cross station**

Stag Place, Victoria, London

Richard Horden Associates

Richard Horden's design for a new High-Tech office block in Victoria as part of a major redevelopment of Stag Place, an ungainly, yet intriguing, example of late 1950s urban renewal. Masterminded by Howard, Fairbairn and Partners in 1959, Stag Place has the air of a quarter around the main railway station in some Eastern European capital. Horden's design for a delicate, almost transparent office tower on the site will raise the standard of architecture here immeasurably. One of the nice ironies is that the new building will be near Buckingham Palace. Prince Charles, scourge of Modernism, must feel grateful that, until crowned king, he lives in Kensington Palace. But which will be better to look at, the new developer's 'luxury apartments' being built alongside Kensington Palace or Horden's finely thought-out tower? The new building which occupies a strategic corner site in central London is due for completion in 1991.

View from Royal Mews

Spitalfields Market redevelopment, Spitalfields, London

Leon Krier

When Spitalfields Market was scheduled to move several miles north in the late 1980s, developers were quick to propose new plans for an area which promised to be a lucrative extension to the City. Any new development had to provide low-cost and lettable housing as well as shops, workshops and office space. Juggling the various scales of buildings required was obviously going to be difficult and so the developers – London and Edinburgh and Rosehaugh Stanhope – turned to some of Britain's most inventive architects for planning and design solutions that would enable them to develop the site to what they saw as its full potential.

Perhaps the most remarkable plan suggested by a commercial developer in the 1980s was that proposed by the uncompromising theorist Leon Krier for Rosehaugh Stanhope. Krier's plan was to re-create a network of city streets complete with crescents and squares fronted with a stern Classical architecture that would create a bridge between the lofty commercial architecture of the City and the exquisite early-Georgian streets of Spitalfields. Krier's idea of the city is a thoroughly European one of close-knit densities and traditional street patterns. However, such architectural altruism rarely finds favour and the Krier scheme disappeared quietly. Spitalfields Market has still, thankfully, to move north.

Project for the redevelopment of Spitalfields Market as drawn by Leon Krier

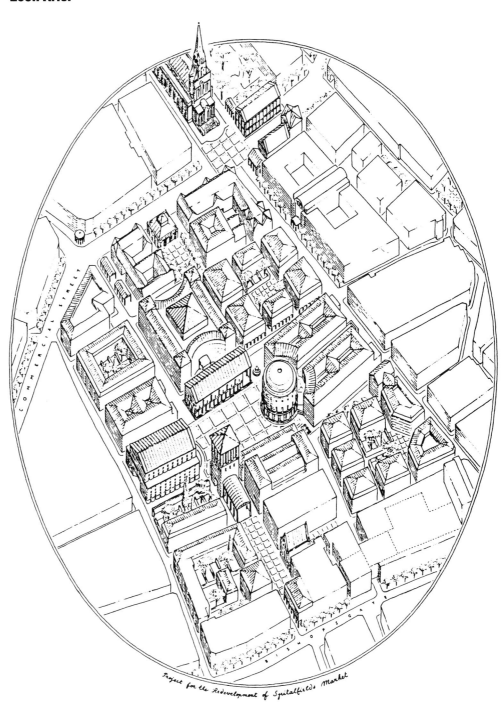

Project for the Redevelopment of Spitalfields Market

175

Horselydown Square, Southwark, London

Wickham Associates

Horselydown from the south end of Tower Bridge, nearing completion

Horselydown Square, begun in 1987, is Julyan Wickham's first built urban-planning project. Occupying a site immediately south-east of Tower Bridge, this is a mixed development of housing, commercial and retail space enclosed in distinctive blue and red protective walls. The architecture is in dramatic contrast to the surrounding warehouses of Butler's Wharf (currently being redeveloped), not least in terms of colour. Wickham's buildings stand out. They also follow a completely different architectural aesthetic from the existing buildings. Horselydown is a distinctly Modern scheme owing much to current Dutch influences. But, being beside the river, it also enjoys a slightly nautical flavour. This is not strait-laced Modern architecture: with its curves, towers, roof-top lookouts and bright colouring, it is decidedly cheerful, and yet it owes precious little to mainstream architectural fads. From the Tower Bridge approach the buildings offer a lively roofscape. In terms of urban planning, they offer protected and quiet space in a noisy area.

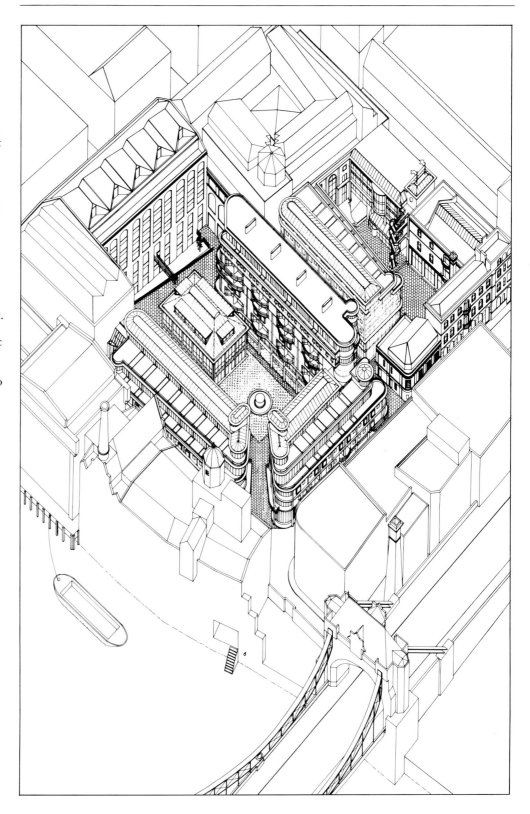

Entrance to Horselydown Square from Tower Bridge

Canary Wharf, Docklands, London
Skidmore, Owings and Merrill

Looking east across the Isle of Dogs. New development is dominated by Cesar Pelli's 850-foot stainless-steel tower

Canary Wharf is one of the biggest building developments in Europe. It is characterized by its remarkable bulk and transatlantic character. This vast complex of City overspill offices and shops will be dominated by an 850-foot office tower designed by the American architect Cesar Pelli, thus creating the tallest commercial building in Europe. It is highly controversial for the way in which it will change dramatically the famous views from Greenwich Park over the City and central London. SOM has created a mini-Manhattan or Chicago skyline characterized by weighty neo-Edwardian and Art Deco style *palazzi*. The landscaping of this City on the water, linked to central London by the Docklands Light Railway, is being designed in consultation with Sir Roy Strong.

King's Cross redevelopment and Broadgate, London

The potential for redevelopment of the industrial wasteland to the north of **King's Cross** station has long been obvious to property developers. **Foster Associates'** controversial plan, revised in October 1988, was sweeping. It envisioned the bridging over of the existing St Pancras Road with the proposed new Channel Tunnel rail terminus and the creation of a new commercial and residential development around an oval park with a lake at its centre. Historic buildings would be moved to new locations around the park. While the plan is undergoing discussion, it is only possible to guess at the architecture that will result.

Broadgate, a fourteen-phase scheme of offices, shops and other commercial activities is still under construction. The first four stages were designed by **Arup Associates**. Later phases are by Skidmore, Owings and Merrill. SOM were chosen for their unrivalled experience in putting up steel-framed buildings to very tight timetables. Broadgate has revolutionized city architecture in Britain. Steel-framed buildings boasting lofty floor-to-ceiling heights to cope with air conditioning and new technology, clad in fanciful polished granite façades, will be the architectural cliché of the 1990s.

Top Foster Associates' master plan, October 1988

Right Office by Arup Associates overlooks open-air public auditorium

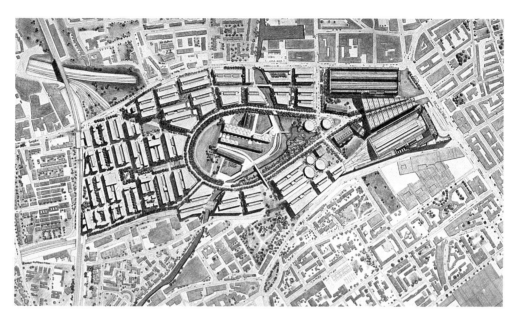

179

Gamester Kenyon, Southwark, London

Harper Mackay

View from street, railway viaduct behind, Southwark Cathedral in the distance

This scheme for the remodelling of a small Victorian office (1988) is a fine example of how new accommodation can be grafted on to old buildings without the architects having to resort to historical pastiche. What matters is a sensitivity to the nature of the street, its character and the views along it. The steel-and-glass upper storeys provide new offices grouped around a large void. These are on an axis with the elevated railway that crosses the Thames here and provide dramatic views of both the Gothic Southwark Cathedral and the Baroque St Paul's. The metalwork enlivening the existing Victorian façade is designed to tie the old and new storeys of the remodelled building together. Although the building is distinctly Modern, what most pedestrians will see are the curved copper roof and decorative clock jutting out into the street.

Epilogue

The 1980s have been remarkable for the revival of public interest in architecture. The media has given increasing attention to new buildings and developments, culminating in Prince Charles's candid television film *Visions of Britain* made by Christopher Martin for the BBC and broadcast in October 1988. Prince Charles attacked the last vestiges of Modernism, tilting his regal lance at, by now, familiar targets: office blocks and high-rise housing. The Prince struck a popular chord in his plea for Classical, Neo-Vernacular and Community Architecture.

It is no wonder that architecture has become a focus of national debate. The astonishing building boom that has characterized Mrs Thatcher's 'enterprise' economy has encouraged a concern for the look of the towns and cities we are creating. Although a number of high-quality buildings by imaginative architects such as John Outram, Norman Foster, Richard Horden and Jeremy Dixon are under construction for developers, most of the new architecture is just as thoughtless as that put up so quickly in the last era of property speculation twenty years ago. The retail boom, a result of tax cuts, instant credit and high consumer expectations, has spawned vast shopping malls that have barged their ungainly way into the heart of every medium-sized British town. The architecture has been, to date, uniformly bad.

Office developments, particularly in London, are being built on an unprecedented scale. American practices such as Skidmore, Owings and Merrill, Kohn Pedersen Fox and Cesar Pelli are giving London a new Post-Modern and transatlantic face. The colossal Broadgate development at Liverpool Street and the giant Canary Wharf scheme on the Isle of Dogs are powerful evidence of this recent trend. Media interest has grown as buildings loom larger and become more adventurous in their surface design.

Considerable public debate followed in the wake of a scheme announced for the complete rebuilding of the Paternoster Square site adjacent to St Paul's Cathedral, a project which has considerably boosted public interest in architecture and town planning. The original outline presented for public inspection in 1987 by Arup Associates met with little understanding. The architects' plans were sketchy and unclear to the layman. Playing on this confusion, the Neo-Classical architect John Simpson stepped in with lovingly drawn and painted perspectives showing how Wren's great dome could float serenely once again above small buildings and narrow streets. His design won the approval of the London *Evening Standard* newspaper and, more importantly, the enthusiastic support of the Prince of Wales.

Simpson's supporters felt that here was a chance to rebuild a part of London that had been spoilt by insensitive redevelopment in the 1950s. Could developers' lust for short-term profit be contained by an appeal for beauty and civic pride in one relatively small, yet powerfully symbolic, part of the nation's capital? When the Arup scheme was presented for public scrutiny in November 1988, it looked as if the architects had come to terms with a Modern architecture imbued with the spirit, if not the language, of Classicism. The new Arup scheme showed a more traditional approach to urban planning in its use of squares and crescents, stone and brick. Sensitive architects such as Michael Hopkins and Richard MacCormac were invited to design some of the individual buildings on the site. The idea of employing a range of architects better known for their design, rather than their financial or marketing skills, is one that developers have taken up in the 1980s as concern for good design has begun to be expressed.

The apotheosis of the appeal to popular taste in the 1980s, is Quinlan Terry's Neo-Classical design for the riverfront buildings at Richmond-upon-Thames. Although critics have complained that Terry's conventional, air-conditioned office interiors are at odds with his provincial eighteenth-century exteriors, public support has given the new Classicists all the vindication they need. The new Richmond scheme has been adopted with evident pleasure by local residents. Terry's riverside terraces are bustling with pleasurable activity in a way that Modern town-planning schemes have always promised in developers' and estate agents' illustrations and yet have failed to achieve.

Public opinion has also applauded the destruction of the architectural heritage of the 1960s. However, there has been no guarantee that replacement schemes will be more elegant. Plans revealed in 1988 to replace the hideous Bull Ring development in the centre of Birmingham by a glitzy commercial, retail and leisure complex on an even larger scale were proof that the purging of old sins did not turn developers and commercial architects into saints and angels. The style of the architecture might change, perhaps slightly for the better, yet the ruthlessly commercial spirit that lies at its foundations remains much the same as it was in the 1960s.

Yet, the realization that many of the landmarks of post-war architecture are under threat of destruction has caused a new generation of pressure groups to champion Brutalist buildings that have never been popular. Architects who once applauded as stripped-down, short-lived buildings

replaced years of great architecture and irreplaceable craft skills, are now shedding crocodile tears over the destruction of such savage monuments to 1960s urban planning as Erno Goldfinger's Elephant and Castle development in south-east London. As if to prove that much Modern thinking was out of tune with ordinary people, the architectural profession stressed the importance of the *ideas* behind Goldfinger's exercise in cold-hearted abstraction. The *reality* was unimportant. Too many Modern buildings have made themselves easy prey for Post-Modern iconoclasts because they were designed on drawing boards for exhibitions and magazines and not as crafted, elevating backdrops to everyday life. In the meantime, more sensitive monuments of their time such as the *Economist* buildings in St James's Street, London, designed by Peter and Alison Smithson, have been listed as worthy of preservation under a change in government ruling. Ironically, the buildings of the heroic period of Brutal British Modernism, the age when only the new was worth having, have themselves become historic fragments that need saving from the ravages of the Post-Modern building boom.

Modernism, however, is far from dead. Norman Foster continues to spearhead a school of architecture that has loosely been labelled 'High Tech', while a younger generation of architects, such as Foster's former assistant David Chipperfield, is developing a new brand of Modernism, one that links the Bauhaus and Le Corbusier to the second machine age. Foster's best work, like that of the other leading British Modernists, Richard Rogers and James Stirling, has been abroad.

Perhaps it is only natural for the British public to be suspicious of a return to Modernism. In Britain, unlike Barcelona, Berlin, Chicago or Paris, the public has only very rarely been exposed to Modern architecture of real quality. This fact has partly been a question of patronage. Most large-scale, new British buildings serve to pay the highest possible financial return as quickly as possible to private developers. Such is the nature of property development. In France successive presidents and mayors of individual towns have sought to leave their mark on posterity by commissioning grand civic buildings, not from tame developers' architects, but from the best architects available. The result is Modern architecture of a quality virtually unknown on this side of the Channel. When presented with a building of real imagination, such as the new Lloyd's headquarters in the City of London, by Richard Rogers and Partners, or Michael Hopkins's Schlumberger building outside Cambridge, the British public reacts with a mixture of awe and disbelief.

Other architects like John Outram have presented an alternative way forward. Outram's recent buildings have begun to demonstrate how ancient themes and traditional ideas of decoration and representation can fuse naturally with buildings housing sophisticated technology and people with a fresh set of needs. Outram's architecture is an imaginative attempt at synthesizing Modernism and Classicism, myth and reality, although his consistent use of vivid polychromy is as demanding on the eye as the work of great British Victorian architects such as William Butterfield and George Edmund Street.

The avant-garde architecture of the 1980s has been the profession's equivalent of the pop video, a rapid sequence of fashionable and eminently publishable images based on a garbled philosophy. This collagist or 'Deconstructivist' approach is concerned with reassembling fragmented ideas and details of the most radical twentieth-century architectural styles and manifestos.

Equally there are a number of young practices, most notably David Chipperfield and Partners, but including others like Pawson Silvestrin, who have reacted against the formal excesses of the 1980s. Their

work is in some ways a return to Modernist forms, if not ideals, and is free from the design clutter found in the buildings of Post-Modern architects.

One area, however, has seen little change in the 1980s. Despite the advance of women in most other professions and walks of life, architecture has remained a largely male occupation. This situation seems set to alter very slowly, partly as a result of the difficulties women experience in dealing with male-dominated building and engineering trades. Eva Jiricna (who trained in her native Czechoslovakia), Zaha Hadid (an Iraqui, who trained at the Architectural Association and who is well known for her stunning Neo-Constructivist drawings) and Eldred Evans appear to be the only women architects based in Britain who have made an international mark in the 1980s.

The major change in the 1980s has been a political one. The shift in patronage from the public to the private sector and the increasing emphasis placed on individual achievement and private wealth have inevitably changed the face of British architecture. The emphasis has shifted irrevocably from an aloof, corporate, consensus Modernism with architects paid from the public purse, to a free-for-all approach adopted by architects surviving in a fiercely competitive world. Although this development has not been welcomed by those opposed to the current government's hard-hearted enterprise economy, it has meant that the 1980s will be remembered as one of the most vibrant decades in British architecture. It is hoped that the buildings and interiors shown in this book demonstrate that the best British architects do not lack imagination or courage. But they need imaginative clients. The more architecture is discussed in Britain, the more likely it is that an architecture of lasting value will result.

Biographies of Architects

Arup Associates

Arup Associates is a multi-disciplinary practice composed of architects, engineers, surveyors and other professionals related to the building process. The practice was formed in 1963 by the engineer Ove Arup and the architect Philip Dowson. Arup Associates' work has been characterized by its strictly Modern idiom.

Major projects include numerous university buildings, Lloyd's offices in Chatham (1983), and offices at Broadgate (1986) in the City of London. 1 Finsbury Avenue (1984) is a key building in the British office building boom of the late 1980s, breaking away from the conventional plan of post-war office blocks.

Ove Arup

Born 1895, Newcastle upon Tyne, died 1988, London. Studied philosophy, mathematics and civil engineering. Set up Arup and Arup (1938), Ove Arup and Partners (1949) and Arup Associates (1963). Worked with Lubetkin and Tecton in the 1930s; founding member of MARS Group (Modern Architectural Research Group) in 1933. Engineered Hunstanton school (1949-54), Sydney Opera House (1956-74), Pompidou Centre (1971-77), among many overtly Modern buildings.

Building Design Partnership

Building Design Partnership was founded by Professor Sir George Grenfell Baines in 1936. The first office of what is now the largest multi-disciplinary architectural practice in Britain was in Preston, Lancashire. Today BDP has nine offices in London, Preston, Guildford, Glasgow, Sheffield and Belfast with a total of 1,500 architects, designers, engineers, planners and cost consultants. The partnership designs a vast range of buildings and interiors, ranging from banks, shopping malls, town centre redevelopments, to light fittings and door catches. BDP adopts current architectural styles quickly, adapting them to major commercial developments. The Ealing Centre (1985) is a fascinating response to a revival of traditional vernacular styles in a busy urban centre.

Campbell Zogolovitch Wilkinson and Gough
Piers Gough

Born 1946, Brighton, Sussex. Trained at the Architectural Association, London (1965-71). Piers Gough worked as an independent architect before setting up in practice as Campbell Zogolovitch Wilkinson and Gough in 1975. He maintains a high media profile as a popular lecturer, writer and broadcaster.

Rex Wilkinson

Born 1947, Skipton, Yorkshire. Trained at the Architectural Association, London (1965-71). Rex Wilkinson worked with a commercial practice for a year before restoring a castle and teaching at the Polytechnic of Central London. He joined his current partners in 1975.

CZWG worked on a large number of house and office extensions and conversions in the mid- and late 1970s, including the fashionable *Time Out* offices in Covent Garden. Since then the practice, which has considerable experience in housing, has grown considerably. Projects during the 1980s include Sutton Square, Eaton Terrace, Orchard Mews and Wolfe Crescent in London's East End and Docklands as well as major apartment blocks at China Wharf, Bermondsey (1985-88), and Cascades on the Isle of Dogs (1986-88). Among their other Docklands schemes under construction are the Circle at Tower Bridge and Jacob's Island in Bermondsey. Outside London, CZWG has designed industrial offices at Aztec West, Bristol (1987) and replanned the centre of Tadcaster. CZWG's work is easily recognizable – flamboyant, cinematic and baroque, earning the architects the title 'English Extremists'.

David Chipperfield

Born 1953, London. Trained at Kingston Polytechnic (1972-74) and the Architectural Association, London (1974-77).

Worked with Douglas Stephens and Partners, Richard Rogers and Partners, the Royal College of Art Project Office and Foster Associates before establishing David Chipperfield and Partners in 1984. Assisted in the design of the Lloyd's headquarters (1978-86) for Richard Rogers and Partners and designed the practice's new offices in Hammersmith. With Foster Associates Chipperfield worked on the design of the Hongkong and Shanghai Bank and the unbuilt BBC headquarters in London.

Recent work includes the Arnolfini Gallery, Bristol; numerous shops for the Japanese fashion guru Issey Miyake in London and in several locations in Japan and the WG shop, selling the latest in modern craft and design in Kensington. The practice is currently working on a private museum in Tokyo, a hotel in Yokohama, an office building in central London and the master plan of the King's Cross redevelopment with Foster Associates. When not shuttling between London and Tokyo, David Chipperfield is also a visiting tutor at the Royal College of Art and a director of the 9H gallery, the only London gallery that specializes in shows of contemporary international architecture. Chipperfield's approach to architecture represents a reappraisal of Modernism, although he is also considerably influenced by traditional Japanese buildings.

Nigel Coates

Born 1949, Malvern, Worcestershire. Trained at the University of Nottingham and the Architectural Association, London (qualified, 1975).

Nigel Coates has taught at the Architectural Association (AA) since 1975. He formed Branson Coates Architecture (BCA) with fellow ex-AA graduate Doug Branson in 1985. His first completed building was a house for fashion designer Jasper Conran (1984-85). Major work since the formation of BCA includes the Jasper Conran shop, London (1985), the Metropole restaurant, Tokyo (1985), Caffe Bongo, Tokyo (1987), the Bohemia nightclub, Tokyo (1986), the Silver shop, London (1987), Noah's Ark restaurant, Tokyo (1988) and the Katharine Hamnett shop, London (1988). Current projects are a mixed-purpose building, the Nishi Wall, Tokyo and the Hotel Maritimo, Otaru, Japan. Probably the most fashionable British architect of the moment, Coates has proved in Japan, and now in Britain, that architecture can be outlandish, humorous as well as highly crafted and designed to last. Through his teaching and his NATO (Narrative Architecture Today) group, Coates has gained a major following among young architects. Having expected to produce architecture on paper only for the rest of his life, Coates is amazed at his own success.

Colquhoun and Miller
Alan Colquhoun
Born 1921, Edinburgh, Scotland. Trained at Edinburgh College of Art (1939-42) and the Architectural Association, London (1947-49).

Alan Colquhoun has had a distinguished career teaching architecture. Principal posts have included: tutor at the Architectural Association (1957-64); principal lecturer for the Polytechnic of Central London (1976-78) and Professor of Architecture at Princeton University (1978 to date). He has taught and examined in many architectural schools and is the author of several volumes of architectural criticism. He set up practice with John Miller in 1961.
John Miller
Born 1930, London. Trained at the Architectural Association,

London (1951-56).
Worked with Lyons Israel Ellis (1956-59) and with Leslie Martin (1959-61). Senior partners in the Colquhoun and Miller practice are Su Rogers (b. 1939) and Richard Brearley (b. 1944). The practice has made a name for its highly rational Modern style in such schemes as a pair of town houses in Camden Town (1983) and the remodelling of the Whitechapel Art Gallery, London (1985). Current projects include a new faculty building for the Royal College of Art, London, a master plan for the redevelopment of the Tate Gallery, London, and new housing in the historic centre of Alcoy, Spain.

Pierre d'Avoine
Born 1951, Bombay, India. Trained at Birmingham School of Architecture (1969-75).

Worked for the Peter Bond partnership (1975-77), the Fitzroy Robinson Partnership (1977-79) and with Powell-Tuck and Connor before setting up in private practice in 1979.

Projects include the Video Post Production building, Camden Town (1982-84) with Powell-Tuck and Connor, a shop for the Japanese fashion designer Michiko Koshino, Soho (1984-85), studio houses in Richmond, Surrey (1987-88), newspaper offices for Dimbleby Newspapers, Richmond, Surrey (1987), and, currently, a new chain of menswear shops for Michiko Koshino in Japan. D'Avoine is able to balance what is fashionable in architecture and design with a more lasting and essentially Modern approach. 'In an increasingly fragmented world,' d'Avoine says, 'it is necessary to make architecture that offers a sense of order amidst the chaos. The paradox is that very often architects are

asked to deal only with the fragments.'

Jeremy Dixon
Born 1939, Bishop's Stortford, Hertfordshire. Trained at the Architectural Association, London (1958-64). Worked for Peter and Alison Smithson, Frederick Macmanus and Partners, Peter and Alison Smithson and Milton Keynes Development Corporation before setting up in private practice in 1973 with Fenella Dixon.

Since 1983 Jeremy Dixon has been designing the Royal Opera House extension in London (in association with the Building Design Partnership). Over the past decade he has completed three distinctive housing schemes in London which marry Classical, historic and Modern traditions. These are St Mark's Road, North Kensington (1975-80), Lanark Road, Maida Vale (1982), and Dudgeon's Wharf, Isle of Dogs (1986-88). Dixon has also designed the coffee shop (1981-82) and restaurant (1984) for the Tate Gallery and the shop at Clifton Nurseries, Maida Vale (1984). A committed urbanist, Dixon has found favour with modern architects as well as the Prince of Wales.

Terry Farrell
Born 1938, Sale, Cheshire. Trained at Durham University School of Architecture (1956-61) and the School of Fine Art, University of Pennsylvania (1962-64).

Terry Farrell worked in partnership with Nicholas Grimshaw from 1965 to 1980. He set up the Terry Farrell Partnership in 1980. The practice has grown rapidly in the 1980s, designing a considerable number of buildings in London. As chairman of the Urban Design Group, Farrell is particularly

concerned with contextual issues. Currently several of his largest-ever buildings are beginning to emerge from under the scaffolding. These include the redevelopment of Charing Cross station and the construction of Alban Gate, a vast Post-Modern office block straddling London Wall.

Major buildings of the past decade include the headquarters for TV-am (1982), television studios in Limehouse (1984), the headquarters for the Henley Royal Regatta (1983-85), the restoration and redevelopment of thirty-two listed buildings in Covent Garden for Comyn Ching and a water treatment works for the Thames Water Authority at Reading, Berkshire (1979-82). Farrell has also made numerous suggestions for the sensitive commercial redevelopment of difficult sites in London, including his best known for London Transport at Hammersmith, and has played a hand in the design of a dramatic house, a Post-Modern manifesto, for the champion of Post-Modern architecture, Charles Jencks (1979-80). Farrell is probably Britain's most committed Post-Modernist, making use of sometimes outlandish colour and decorative devices in his unmistakable buildings. He has been greatly influenced by American Art Deco and the American Post-Modern architect, Michael Graves.

Faulkner-Brown, Watkinson, Hendy and Stonor
This practice, based in Newcastle upon Tyne, was established in 1962 by Harry Faulkner-Brown (born 1924, Newcastle), Ernie Watkinson (born 1937, Newcastle; qualified 1960), Stuart Hendy (born 1936, Newcastle) and Bill Stonor (born 1938,

Newcastle; qualified 1961). The partners were all educated at the University of Durham School of Architecture. Harry Faulkner-Brown retired in 1984 when the practice changed its name to Faulkner-Browns and took on a new partner – Neil Taylor (born 1951, Leeds, Yorkshire; qualified 1976 from the University of Sheffield School of Architecture).

The practice specializes in leisure centres, sports halls and tourist facilities, but has also designed such key civic buildings in the north of England as the civic centre at Chester-le-Street (1983). The practice has no conscious house style, but differs from most established commercial practices by following any given approach to architecture with conviction. Current major projects include the design of the Ponds Forge international sports and leisure complex, Sheffield, which will open in 1991 to coincide with the World Student Games (Universiad), the 350-acre Doncaster leisure park and a major inner-city redevelopment plan for central Birmingham.

Norman Foster

Born 1935, Manchester. Educated at the University of Manchester and the Yale University of Architecture. Formed Team 4 in 1963 with his wife Wendy, and Su and Richard Rogers. Foster Associates was started in 1967.

Foster works at the leading edge of building technology. His buildings owe much of their elegance and detailing to aircraft, automotive and marine design. His High-Tech architecture is often described as Classical in its ordered serenity as opposed to his ex-partner Richard Rogers whose 'Bowellist' approach to buildings, such as the Lloyd's

headquarters in the City of London (1978-86), has been labelled High-Tech Gothic. Foster's most important buildings include the passenger terminal and administration building at Fred Olsen Lines, London (1971), the Willis, Faber and Dumas office, Ipswich, Suffolk (1975), the Sainsbury Centre for the Visual Arts at the University of East Anglia (1978), the Renault distribution centre, Swindon, Wiltshire (1983) and the Hongkong and Shanghai Banking Corporation headquarters, Hong Kong (1979-86). At present Foster is working on an office tower in Tokyo, the design of the Bilbao Metro system, Spain, a communications tower in Barcelona, Spain, a new headquarters for ITN in Bloomsbury, London, and the Médiathèque arts centre in Nîmes, France. Foster was awarded the Royal Gold Medal for Architecture in 1983.

Barry Gasson

Born 1935, Westcliffe-on-Sea, Essex. Trained at Birmingham School of Architecture and Columbia University, New York (1959-61).

After qualifying from Columbia, Gasson taught at Cambridge University before winning the competition for the design of a museum to house the Burrell Collection outside Glasgow. From 1971 to 1983 Gasson worked on his own, setting up a practice in Glasgow to commit himself to this major project. Gasson's approach to the design of this eclectic collection from a Glaswegian shipping magnate was to marry a formal Modern plan to a romantic elevation and roofscape. Employing both new and traditional materials, Gasson has created a populist Modern Movement building. He is currently working on new

housing developments and is Visiting Professor at Manchester School of Architecture.

Nicholas Grimshaw

Born 1939, London. Trained at Edinburgh College of Art and the Architectural Association, London (qualified 1965). Nick Grimshaw set up in private practice with Terry Farrell in 1965 and in his own right in 1980.

Major work with Terry Farrell includes Park Road apartments, London (1968), a factory for Hermann Miller, Bath (1976), and factory units at Warrington (1978). Since 1980 Grimshaw's principal projects have been: the headquarters for BMW, Bracknell (1980), a furniture factory for Vitra, Germany (1981), an ice rink at Oxford (1985), Sainsbury's supermarket, Camden Town (1988), the printing works for the *Financial Times* (1988). At present Grimshaw is designing the North Woolwich pumping station in the London Docklands and the Channel Tunnel terminal at Waterloo.

Grimshaw's ancestors have included several generations of engineers on his father's side and artists on his mother's. Grimshaw himself is an architect with a passion for engineering. At their best, his buildings capture and extend the excitement of high Victorian engineering. His heroes include Joseph Paxton, Gustav Eiffel and Isambard Kingdom Brunel.

Harper Mackay
David Harper

Born 1956, Johnstone, Scotland. Trained at the Mackintosh School of Architecture (1974-80). Worked for Spence and Webster Architects and Nicholas Grimshaw and

Partners before setting up in private practice in 1984.

Kenneth Mackay

Born 1959, Glasgow, Scotland. Trained at the Canterbury College of Art (1976-78) and the Royal College of Art (1978-80). Worked for Jeremy Dixon before joining David Harper.

Richard Knowles

Born 1952, Sowerby Bridge, West Riding, Yorkshire. Trained at Brighton Polytechnic (1970-73) and the Royal College of Art (1974-77). Before joining Harper Mackay, Knowles worked with Jeremy Dixon and Douglas Stephen and Partners.

After qualifying as an architect, David Harper was responsible for many buildings, ranging from schools and hospitals to sports halls and an ice rink, while Ken Mackay was working with Jeremy Dixon on the winning scheme in the Covent Garden opera house competition. Their disparate skills have brought them a large number of projects in a very short time. Major work includes a mixed residential and industrial development in Maida Vale, London (1988), shops for Goldberg PLC in Manchester, Glasgow, Chester among other places (1988), a factory for an American hair-care manufacturer in Basildon (1988), new work at Clifton Nurseries, London (1984-88), many house and office conversions, and work for both Jeremy Dixon and Nicholas Grimshaw.

Michael Hopkins

Born 1935, Poole, Dorset. Trained at the Architectural Association, London (1959-62). Worked with Leonard Manassah and Partners (1963-65), Tom Hancock (1966-68) and Foster Associates (1969-75).

Michael Hopkins and Partners was formed in 1976.

Since starting his own practice, Hopkins has designed several of the most convincing High-Tech buildings in Britain from his own house in Hampstead, London in 1976, to the Mound Stand at Lord's Cricket Ground for the Marylebone Cricket Club in 1987. Notable buildings in between include the Greene King brewery, Bury St Edmunds (1979) and the Schlumberger Research Laboratories, Cambridge (1985). His most recent projects have included a cutlery factory for David Mellor at Hathersage, Derbyshire (1988) and the redevelopment of Bracken House, the ex-*Financial Times* building in the City of London. Hopkins's buildings are characterized by the use of modern tent structures (as at Schlumberger and Lord's) and, recently, by the fusion of contemporary design and traditional materials (as at Lord's and the Mellor factory).

Richard Horden

Born 1944, Hereford. Trained at the Architectural Association, London (1964-69).

Worked with the Farrell Grimshaw Partnership (1971-72), Spence and Webster (1972-74) and Foster Associates (1974-84) before setting up Richard Horden Associates in 1985. After being involved in some of the key High-Tech projects of the 1970s and early 1980s, including the Sainsbury Centre for the Visual Arts (1978) and the Hongkong and Shanghai Bank (1979-86) for Foster Associates, Richard Horden has gone on to build several distinguished private houses based on current boat technology. He has also built homes for craft workers in Dorset, an extension to Bryanston school, yacht club

houses, a marina control tower and a swimming pool. His major project in 1989 is a new office tower in Victoria, London. His architecture is characterized by its uncompromising Modernism, logical construction and great clarity.

Eva Jiricna

Born 1938, Prague, Czechoslovakia. Trained at the University of Prague. Qualified in 1963 from the Academy of Fine Arts, Prague.

Eva Jiricna came to London in 1968. In Prague she had worked for the Institute of Building and Interior Design. In London she designed schools for the Greater London Council before joining the Louis de Soissons Partnership as an associate in 1969. She set up in partnership with David Hodges in 1980 before leaving in 1982 to establish her own practice. Jiricna Kerr Associates was formed in 1985 and Eva Jiricna Architects in 1987. Her best known work includes Le Caprice restaurant, Mayfair (1981), Joe's Café, Brompton Cross (1985), Legends nightclub, Mayfair (1985), interiors of Lloyd's headquarters, London (1985-86), and several shops for the fashion retailer Joseph Ettedgui, including the new Joseph shop at Brompton Cross (1988). Among her projects in progress are a shop for the Danish furriers Birger Christensen in Copenhagen, a chain of retail outlets for shoe designers Joan and David in the USA, Britain and Canada, a flat for the Thompson Twins and an office in Switzerland for the furniture manufacturer Vitra. Jiricna's highly polished, often monochrome, interiors are instantly recognizable. Very durable, they seem to be permanent additions to the architectural scene.

Leon Krier

Born 1946, Luxembourg. Trained briefly at the Technische Hochschule, Stuttgart.

Worked with James Stirling (1968-70) and J. P. Kleihues (1971-72) before setting up private practice in London in 1974. Krier is a polemicist and a clever draughtsman who campaigns through his drawings, writing and teaching for a return to the pre-industrial city. His chosen architectural style, a rational early nineteenth-century Classicism, has often been compared unfavourably with the work of Albert Speer (1905-81), of whom he published a major study in 1983. His redesign of Luxembourg City (1978) and his scheme for the redevelopment of Spitalfields Market (1987) have helped to make architects, developers and politicians rethink their positions on urban design issues. At present he is working on the design of a new village near Dorchester, Dorset, for the Duchy of Cornwall.

Richard MacCormac

Born 1938, London. Trained at the University of Cambridge (qualified 1962) and University College, London (1963-65). Worked for Powell and Moya, Lyons Israel Ellis and the London Borough of Merton. He has been in private practice since 1969 and formed MacCormac Jamieson in 1972.

Major projects include university buildings at Oxford, Cambridge and Bristol, housing in Duffryn, South Wales and Milton Keynes. At present he is working on the redevelopment of Spitalfields Market, London with the Fitzroy Robinson Partnership. MacCormac's work is distinctive for being true to the tenets of Modernism, though it uses traditional and natural

materials. It shows that Modernism could have been well received in Britain, if only buildings had been softer in focus and less brutal. Richard MacCormac is a teacher and writer and a member of the Royal Fine Art Commission.

Rick Mather

Born 1937, Portland, Oregon, USA. Trained at the University of Oregon (qualified 1961) and the Architectural Association, London (1961-67). Worked for Lyons Israel Ellis and the London Borough of Southwark on housing schemes. Taught at the Architectural Association, the Bartlett School of Architecture and the Polytechnic of Central London. Set up own practice in 1972.

Mather's most notable buildings include the Peter Eaton bookshop, Holland Park (1974), the renovation of the Architectural Association, Bedford Square (1977-82), a house in Eaton Villas, London (1979-81), a computer science building for the Schools of Information Studies and Education, University of East Anglia (1981-85), and Zen W3 (1985) and Zen Central (1987), Chinese restaurants in Hampstead and Mayfair. At present he is working on a housing complex in Khartoum, a new Zen restaurant in Hong Kong and a development plan for the University of East Anglia. An uncompromising Modernist, Mather's buildings and interiors lose none of their appeal or glitter over the years. While tower blocks of the same period begin to tumble, the Peter Eaton bookshop, built to a very tight budget, remains up to the minute and unchanged despite new ownership.

John Outram

Born 1934, Malaysia. Trained at the Polytechnic of Central London, and the Architectural

Association, London (qualified 1961).

John Outram worked in housing and town planning with the Greater London Council and with the Fitzroy Robinson Partnership before remodelling Nash villas and terraces in Regent's Park for the Louis de Soissons Partnership. He set up private practice in 1973. After a spell of routine kitchen and bathroom extensions, Outram began significant building in 1976 with a series of warehouses at Poyle, Middlesex and later, in 1982, at Kensal Road, London. Major projects since then have included the headquarters for Harp Central Heating at Swanley, Kent (1984), a reskinning of steel and concrete offices dating from the 1960s, industrial warehouses and offices at Aztec West, Bristol (1987), a country house at Wadhurst, East Sussex (1986), and a pumping station for the London Docklands Development Corporation on the Isle of Dogs (1988). He is currently working on an office building in the City of London.

An ex-Royal Canadian Air Force pilot, Outram flirted with High-Tech in the late 1950s and early 1960s. Since then he has invented and developed a fascinating language of architecture that is entirely his own. 'Architecture', says Outram, perhaps Britain's most inventive architect, 'is not graphics, it is not the play of pure images, mere names. It is the play of things that have no name, because they cannot be named: the corporalia of concept, the embodiments of thought, the elephants of memory, that fertile fantasy ground where the unconscious and the conscious fuse in the confusion of being. Post-Modern façadism' – of which Outram cannot be accused – 'is iconic, it is pictorial, but that is

architecture recollected, not architecture itself.' Highly articulate, Outram contributes to many architectural magazines and is a popular lecturer.

Pawson Silvestrin
John Pawson
Born 1949, Halifax, Yorkshire. Trained at Nagoya University of Commerce and the Architectural Association, London (1981-83).
Claudio Silvestrin
Born 1954, Milan, Italy. Trained at Milan Polytechnic, University of Bologna and the Architectural Association, London (1984).

John Pawson and Claudio Silvestrin set up in practice together in 1983. They have designed many Minimalist interiors and are now working on a new house in Hampstead. Major projects include the Waddington Galleries, London (1983), the Wakaba restaurant, London (1987) and the Starckmann office, London (1988). Both architects dislike their work being labelled Minimalist, Japanese or Zen. Silvestrin claims that his 'interest in simplicity goes beyond the edge of the drawing board: indeed it pierces every living choice'. Pawson Silvestrin's clear, poetic architecture is remarkable for its stand against decoration and colour. Both believe that white is the purest and most subtle colour available to architects.

Powell-Tuck, Connor and Orefelt
Julian Powell-Tuck
Born 1952, Knowle, West Midlands. Trained at Solihull College of Art, Brighton College of Art and the Royal College of Art, London (1974-76). Set up private practice in 1976.
David Connor
Born 1950, Solihull, West Midlands. Trained at

Birmingham College of Art (1969-73), Royal College of Art, London (1973-76). Worked for Milton Keynes Development Corporation and John Stefanidis (1977-78) as a designer before joining Powell-Tuck in 1979.
Gunnar Orefelt
Born 1953, Stockholm, Sweden. Studied at University of Upsala, Royal Institute of Technology, Stockholm (1974-78) and Architectural Association, London (1978-79). Worked on mass housing schemes with FFNS Architects, Stockholm (1976-78) and with Nilsson Associates, London on housing in Milton Keynes (1979-82). Joined Powell-Tuck and Connor in 1982.

Emerging as architects at the end of the Punk movement in the late 1970s, Powell-Tuck and Connor worked with Vivienne Westwood, Malcolm McClaren and punk musicians before widening their horizons and refining their approach to architecture. In the 1980s, they have produced a considerable number of interiors and houses for developers and now act as their own developers. Major works include the Arrow House in California (1984-88), a house in Battersea, London (1986-87), a mixed-used development in Fulham, London (1987-89), and an artist's studio in Venice, California. David Connor's drawings and paintings have been exhibited in private galleries in Britain and the USA and at the Victoria and Albert Museum, London.

Ian Ritchie
Born 1947, Hove, Sussex. Trained at Liverpool School of Architecture (1965-68) and the Polytechnic of Central London (1970-72). Registered as an architect in Great Britain and France.

Worked for Foster

Associates (1972-76) where he was involved in the design of the Willis, Faber and Dumas office, Ipswich, Suffolk (1972-75) and the Sainsbury Centre for the Visual Arts at the University of East Anglia (1974-76). Worked as an independent architect in Paris before setting up Chrysalis Architects with Michael Dowd and Alan Stanton (1979-81). A director of Rice, Francis, Ritchie, based in Paris from 1981 to 1986. Has also been in private practice as Ian Ritchie Architects based in London since 1981. Taught at the Architectural Association, London (1979-82).

Ritchie's major buildings to date include the Eagle Rock House (1983) and new apartment housing in Docklands (1985-88). He is currently designing the new planetarium in Greenwich, London. Ritchie's work crosses the disciplines of architecture and engineering, as the adventurous design of Eagle Rock House reveals, or even his work on experimental vehicles for Fiat (with Renzo Piano), gantry cranes, high tensile fabric roofs, and the Crocopolis in Nîmes, France, an 'ecological tropical greenhouse for crocodiles'.

John Simpson
Born 1954, Marlborough, Wiltshire. Trained at University of London and the Bartlett School of Architecture (qualified 1979).

A Classical revivalist, Simpson runs his own London practice based opposite Sir Robert Smirke's British Museum. Simpson achieved a high public profile very quickly in 1987 and 1988 with his alternative Classical scheme for Paternoster Square, adjacent to St Paul's Cathedral and a commissioned scheme for London Bridge City II.

Completed work to date includes a house in the style of Sir John Soane in Ashfold, Sussex (1986-89), new telephone boxes for Mercury Communications Ltd (1988) and a design for a new village at Upper Donnington, Berkshire (1989). Simpson believes that 'it is only natural that we should turn to our heritage and tradition and, by building upon that, express ourselves as a society in much the same way as our forefathers always did in the past'.

Skidmore, Owings and Merrill

The London office of SOM was set up in 1986 in response to the London office building boom which resulted from the deregulation of the stock market in autumn of that year. A scion of the giant American practice based principally in New York and Chicago, SOM (London) is currently working on the master plan of the Canary Wharf development on the Isle of Dogs and the planning and design of most phases of the Broadgate development in the City of London. SOM gained a foothold in the lucrative London office market because of the practice's impressive fifty-year track record in designing steel-framed building at great speed in the USA.

SOM was founded in 1939 by Louis Skidmore (1897-1962), Nathaniel Owings (1903-84) and John Merrill (1896-1975). Run on strict business principles from its inception, SOM has stood against the celebration of individual talent in favour of the corporate whole. SOM's first building to receive world-wide acclaim was the Lever House, New York (1952). Since then the practice has worked and reworked the architecture of the early masters of the Modern

Movement (most noticeably Mies van de Rohe). Today SOM has adopted a fashionable Post-Modern Classical look for its city towers.

Stanton and Williams
Alan Stanton
Born 1944, Northampton. Trained at the Architectural Association, London (1962-67) and the University of California, Los Angeles (1969-71).
Paul Williams
Born 1949, Birmingham, West Midlands. Trained at Birmingham College of Art (1969-75) and Yale Arts Centre (1978).

Stanton and Williams made their name in the 1980s with a large number of stunning designs for exhibitions (including 'The Age of Chivalry' at the Royal Academy, London, 1987), for temporary buildings (the medieval-like tents outside the Tate Gallery, London, 1983) and for a shop for the Japanese fashion design Issey Miyake (London, 1987). These projects have led to major commissions, including, currently, the extension of Birmingham City Museums and Art Gallery, the exhibition galleries of the Design Museum at Butler's Wharf, London, and a new wing for the twentieth-century collection of the National Portrait Gallery.

Quinlan Terry
Born 1937, Hampstead, London. Trained at the Architectural Association, London and the British School at Rome (1967).

Quinlan Terry set up practice with Raymond Erith in 1962 after a brief spell as an assistant with Stirling and Gowan. Major projects with Erith included a Suffolk country house at Kingswalden Bury (1970), the New Common

Room Building, Gray's Inn, London (1971), and the restoration of the eighteenth-century church, St Mary's, Paddington Green (1973). Since Erith's death in 1973, Terry has been the torchbearer of revived British Classicism. In the guise of Erith and Terry he has built several country houses from Yorkshire to the Cotswolds and as far afield as Kentucky, Ohio. His most recent work includes the redevelopment of Richmond riverside, Surrey (completed 1988), a project for new Classical villas in Regent's Park, London (1987), and a new building for Downing College, Cambridge (1988). A devout Anglican, Terry is a fierce apostle of the Classical creed. In 1988 he vented his undoubtedly popular opinions on a BBC TV documentary *Visions of Britain*.

Julyan Wickham
Born 1942, Pheale, Berkshire. Trained at the Architectural Association, London (1961-66).

Before studying at the Architectural Association, Julyan Wickham worked for Raglan Squire and Partners. He spent a year in India and Pakistan working on housing, hospital and hotel schemes for William Perry Associates before qualifying. He worked for Edward Cullinan Architects (1966-75) before setting up in private practice. Projects included a conference centre at Minster Lovell, a training centre for British Olivetti, Haslemere, an artist's studio in Marlborough and a bar for Peterhouse, Cambridge.

His own partnership (as Julyan Wickham Architect, Wickham and Baumgarten and Wickham Associates) has designed several fashionable London bars and restaurants starting with Zanzibar, Covent

Garden (1976) and most recently Kensington Place, Notting Hill (1988). Work of the last few years includes local authority housing for the London Borough of Waltham (1988) and Horselydown Square, a mixed urban development of shops, offices and flats on the south-east side of Tower Bridge, London (1987-89). Wickham is an unashamedly Modern architect, whose work proves that Modern architecture can be rich, warm, well crafted and fit into the city without having to ape traditional styles.

David Wild
Born 1938, Portsmouth, Hampshire. Trained at the Southern College of Art, Portsmouth (1956-59) and the Architectural Association, London (1959-62).

Worked on the design of Bentley School, Hampshire, for Lyons Israel Ellis (1962-63), on a Le Corbusier-inspired office building in Watford, Hertfordshire, for Douglas Stephen and Partners (1963-65), with Skidmore, Owings and Merrill in Chicago (1965-67) and for RMJM on the design of university housing at Bath (1967-68). Freelance from 1968. Stopped practising as an architect temporarily to work as a graphic designer and journalist. Published *The Big Red Diary* (1974) and designed the International Socialist Bookshop, London, in 1973. Taught at the Architectural Association and full time at the Gloucester College of Art and Design, Cheltenham, in the 1970s. Now teaches architecture at the Polytechnic of the South Bank. Designed his own house in a Modernist style in 1985. Wild has recently completed a second house in Camden Town (1989) which reinforces his commitment to Modernism.

Select Bibliography

1 *Books on recent British architecture and architectural thinking:*

Albion, Ark, *Architecture by Nigel Coates and the NATO Group* (1987)
Alison + Peter Smithson (1982)
Appleyard, Bryan, *Richard Rogers: A Biography* (1986)
Archer, Lucy, *Raymond Erith: Architect* (1985)
Aslet, Clive, *Quinlan Terry: The Revival of Architecture* (1986)
Banham, Reyner, *Age of the Masters: A Personal View of Modern Architecture* (1975)
Beck, Haig (ed.), *The State of the Art: A Cultural History of British Architecture* (1984)
Cedric Price (1984)
Colquhoun, Alan, *Essays in Architectural Criticism: Modern Architecture and Historical Change* (1981)
Crook, J. Mordaunt, *The Dilemma of Style* (1987)
Cullen, Gordon, *Townscape* (1954)
Curtis, William J. R., *Modern Architecture Since 1900* (1982)
Erno Goldfinger (1983)
Figueiredo, Peter de, and Julian Treuherz, *Cheshire Country Houses* (1988)
Frampton, Kenneth, *Modern Architecture: A Critical History* (1980)
Future Systems: Jan Kapkicky and David Nixon (1987)
Hampshire Architecture (1985)
Jackson, Alan, *The Politics of Architecture* (1970)
Jencks, Charles, *Architecture Today* (1988)
———, *Modern Movements in Architecture* (1973)
———, *Post Modernism* (1970)
———, *Prince Charles and the Architects* (1988)
———, *Symbolic Architecture* (1985)
Johnson, Philip, and Mark Wigley, *Deconstructivist Architecture* (1988)
Lampugnani, Vittorio Magnago (ed.), *The Thames and Hudson Encyclopaedia of 20th-Century Architecture* (1986)
Le Corbusier, *Towards a New Architecutre* (1927)
———, *The Radiant City* (1967)
Loos, Adolf, *Ornament and Crime* (1908)
Lyons Israel Ellis (1988)
Moos, Stanislaus von, *Venturi, Rauch & Scott Brown: Buildings and Projects* (1987)
Nairn, Ian, *Outrage* (1955)
Nicholas Grimshaw and Partners (1988)
Norman Foster 1964-87 (1988)
Papadakis, Andreas (ed.), *Arup: Ove Arup and Partners, 1946-86* (1986)
———, *British Architecture* (1982)
Peter Cook: 21 Years, 21 Ideas (1985)
Pevsner, Nikolaus, *An Outline of European Architecture* (1943)
Porphyrios, Dimetri (ed.), *Leon Krier: Houses, Palaces, Cities* (1982)
Robinson, John Martin, *The Latest Country Houses* (1984)
Ron Herron: 20 Years of Drawings (1980)
Rowe, Colin, *James Stirling: Buildings and Projects* (1984)
Saint, Andrew, *Towards a Social Architecture: The Role of School Building in Post-War England* (1987)
Stern, Robert A. M., *Modern Classicism* (1988)
Sudjic, Deyan, *Norman Foster, Richard Rogers, James Stirling: New Directions in British Architecture* (1986)
Sudjic, Deyan, Peter Cook and Jonathan Meades, *English Eccentrics: The Architecture of Campbell Zogolovitch Wilkinson and Gough* (1988)
Terry Farrell (1984)
Thackara, John (ed.), *Design After Modernism* (1988)
Venturi, Robert, *Complexity and Contradiction in Architecture* (1966)
Walker, Derek, *The Architecture and Planning of Milton Keynes* (1982)
Watkin, David, *Morality and Architecture* (1977)
Wofle, Ivor de, *Civilia or the End of Sub Urban Man* (1971)
Wolfe, Tom, *From Our House to Bauhaus* (1982)
Zaha Hadid: Planetary Architecture (1985)

2 *Magazines on new trends and developments in British architecture:*

a) *The Architect's Journal* (weekly) is a meticulous and sober publication which presents, along with news and reviews, detailed appraisals of new buildings, materials and construction techniques. Concerned with the promotion of excellence in modern architecture, it has also been a powerful voice in the conservation movement.
b) *The Architectural Review* (monthly) dates from 1896 and is the leading British architectural magazine. Its staff has at various times comprised Hubert de Cronin Hastings, John Betjeman, Osbert Lancaster, Nikolaus Pevsner, Peter Reyner Banham and Ian Nairn. International in scope, today's *Architectural Review* concentrates almost exclusively on reviewing buildings and projects by the most significant contemporary architects.
c) *Architectural Design* (ten times a year) is an occasional magazine, normally published as a discursive and well-illustrated monograph on a particular architect, fad or theme.
d) *Blueprint* (ten times a year) is an up-to-the-minute, fashionable monthly broadsheet covering architecture and design. Best known for its powerful graphics, it has lively features aimed at a design-conscious public.
e) *Building Design* (weekly), a newspaper-style broadsheet, is concerned primarily with news, reviews and gossip, though it also runs serious, and often provocative, features.
f) *Transactions* (twice a year) includes lectures given by influential architects and critics at the Royal Institute of British Architects.

Sources of illustrations

Index